EVERYTHING
YOU NEED TO KNOW ABOUT...

DOG TRAINING AND TRICKS

Dear Reader,

My hope in writing the second edition of this book is to further inspire dog lovers everywhere to train their dogs using kind, effective training methods that help maintain a lifelong bond between dogs and their people. My hope is to share with you some of the secrets that can help you train your dog to be a loving companion and polite member of your family. The bonds we have with our canine companions hold us together during the ups and downs of life and provide us with the necessary stability to exist in this sometimes chaotic and fast-paced world we live in. My wish for you is that you will experience the joys of living with a dog that is smart and capable. With the right guidance, your dog will be able to participate in as much of your life as possible. The more well-behaved your dog is, the more places he can go and the more activities he can participate in.

There is no adventure as exciting as training a dog and learning how his mind works and how he communicates. With practice, you will find that dogs are wonderfully intelligent and have a great sense of humor. I have worked with dogs for more than half of my life, and I've taught close to 2,000 people how to train their dogs. I can honestly say that training a dog is a trip you don't want to miss. I hope this book helps you continue on your journey toward training a well-behaved dog and that you have many happy years together.

Happy tails,

Gerilyn J. Bielakiewicz

Welcome to the EVERYTHING YOU NEED TO KNOW ABOUT... series!

These handy, accessible books give you all you need to tackle a difficult project, gain a new hobby, comprehend a fascinating topic, prepare for an exam, or even brush up on something you learned back in school but have since forgotten.

You can choose to read an **EVERYTHING** book from cover to cover or just pick out the information you want from our four useful boxes: e-questions, e-facts, e-alerts, and e-ssentials. We give you everything you need to know on the subject, but throw in a lot of fun stuff along the way, too.

We now have more than 400 **EVERYTHING** books in print, spanning such wide-ranging categories as weddings, pregnancy, cooking, music instruction, foreign language, crafts, pets, New Age, and so much more. When you're done reading them all, you can finally say you know **EVERYTHING**!

QUESTION?
Answers to
common questions

FACTS
Important snippets
of information

ALERTS!
Urgent
warnings

ESSENTIALS
Quick
handy tips

PUBLISHER Karen Cooper

DIRECTOR OF ACQUISITIONS AND INNOVATION Paula Munier

MANAGING EDITOR, EVERYTHING SERIES Lisa Laing

COPY CHIEF Casey Ebert

ACQUISITIONS EDITOR Katie McDonough

DEVELOPMENT EDITOR Elizabeth Kassab

EDITORIAL ASSISTANT Hillary Thompson

Visit the entire **EVERYTHING YOU NEED TO KNOW ABOUT...** series at *www.davidandcharles.co.uk*

EVERYTHING

YOU NEED TO KNOW ABOUT...

Dog Training & Tricks

All you need to turn even the most mischievous
pooch into a well-behaved pet

Gerilyn J. Bielakiewicz, cofounder of Canine University

D&C
David and Charles

For Cameo, our sweet wonderful girl.
The first edition brought you into our lives,
and the second edition kept you here!

First published in the USA in 2009 as *The Everything® Dog Training & Tricks Book* by
Adams Media, an F+W Media Company
57 Littlefield Street, Avon, MA 02322 U.S.A.
www.adamsmedia.com

Photographs copyright © Donna Kelliher

ISBN-13: 978-0-7153-3295-5 paperback
ISBN-10: 0-7153-3295-3 paperback

Printed and bound in Great Britain by CPI Antony Rowe Ltd, Chippenham
Brunel House   Newton Abbot   Devon

Visit our website at www.davidandcharles.co.uk

David & Charles books are available from all good bookshops; alternatively you
can contact our Orderline on 0870 9908222 or write to us at FREEPOST EX2 110,
D&C Direct, Newton Abbot, TQ12 4ZZ (no stamp required UK only);
US customers call 800-289-0963 and Canadian customers call 800-840-5220.

Contents

Acknowledgments

Thank you to my husband, Paul; my children Mark, Eric, and Julia; and my Golden Five: Reggae, Cameo, Tess, Rush, and Bode. You are the inspiration for all that I do.

Top Ten Components of a Happy, Healthy Dog

1. Love and Companionship
2. Just Leadership
3. Safety and Security
4. Sound Nutrition (food, water, and treats)
5. Veterinary Care
6. Exercise
7. Grooming
8. Toys and Games
9. Comfortable Beds
10. Family

Introduction

▶TRAINING YOUR DOG IS a way to establish a line of communication, a common language that you will use to communicate with your dog for her entire lifetime. Whether you spend time teaching your dog simple obedience commands or complicated tricks, you will strengthen your relationship with your dog and build a strong foundation of trust. Developing a trusting relationship with your dog through the use of positive training methods will enhance the special bond that you share with your dog, and it will also make the quality of life you share all the better.

Training is a relationship, and like all relationships it needs to be maintained through lots of repetition and practice. Training has no designated beginning or end since a dog is capable of learning throughout its entire lifetime. Initially, training involves lots of practice and will probably include attending classes to learn how to practice when surrounded by distractions. Eventually, you may not train your dog formally every day, but your dog will still be learning new things every day, and participating in that learning is what owning a dog is all about.

Behavior problems can be detrimental to establishing a relationship with your dog and keeping it strong, and I have addressed several of the most trying ones in this book. The solutions are simple, and they concentrate on rebuilding trust in your relationship with your dog while simultaneously improving your dog's manners and comfort. Almost every behavior problem relates back to some need that has not been met. You will notice a pattern as you read about the solutions to each problem: A lot of dogs would not exhibit behavior problems if they got enough exercise. If your dog is experiencing a behavior problem that is threatening your sanity, consider increasing her daily exercise and see if this helps alleviate the intensity of the problem. The topics covered in this book range from teaching tricks to solving behavior problems, and I hope it inspires you to build a great relationship with your dog and have fun doing it. There is no greater reward for your hard effort than the loyalty and love of a faithful canine companion. Great dog companions—like great human companions—are not born. They are cultivated by spending time together, learning about each other, and learning how to develop the strongest relationship possible. It is my sincere wish that this book will positively change the way you view dog training and enhance your relationship with your dog.

CHAPTER 1

Why Teach Tricks?

Teaching tricks is a must for every dog owner who thinks of her pet as part of the family. Training a dog is like any other relationship; it is partly about establishing rules and boundaries (what is and isn't acceptable), partly about teaching your dog what is expected of him, and partly about spending time together.

Training Improves Your Relationship

From the moment you bring your new puppy into your home, she is learning how to get along with your family, a species entirely different from her own. If your instruction is vague and inconsistent, her confusion about what is acceptable will manifest itself in undesirable behavior and mischief. If you spend time teaching your dog what is expected of her, you will be rewarded with a well-mannered pet that becomes a beloved member of your family. You get what you reinforce. If you pay attention to what your dog is doing right, you'll reap the rewards of a well-behaved dog.

Teaching tricks is about having fun and being a little silly, but it can also greatly benefit a frustrated owner and an overactive dog. Teaching your dog to roll over or play dead may seem a bit frivolous until you realize that to do those tricks your dog must have some basic understanding of the Sit or Lie Down command. Teaching tricks capitalizes and improves upon what the dog already knows and makes it better. A goofy, energetic dog will keep her paws off the company, for instance, if she has a show-stopping Play Dead command in her repertoire. Another benefit of trick training is that it improves public relations—doggie PR—with non–dog lovers.

The beauty of teaching tricks is that they can be taught to any dog of any size, breed, or temperament; you are only limited by the dog's physical ability to perform the task. It's crucial for larger dogs, especially those whose breed alone makes people nervous, to learn some fun and silly tricks that they can do when they meet new people. People will react totally differently to a big silly German shepherd balancing a cookie on her nose than they would to one sitting politely. This also has an added benefit for your dog: The more relaxed visitors are, the more your dog will like having them around.

Trick Training Leads to Better Training

Teaching tricks can help you control a dog that barks too much or shakes and shivers when he meets new people simply by giving him a more acceptable alternative. Trick training will make you a better dog trainer, a person who knows how to motivate her dog and has learned how to break things down into small parts. Since training your dog is a lifelong process, the more you practice the skills of a good dog trainer, the better you will become, and the more quickly your dog will learn.

The most difficult part of being a beginner is that you are learning at the same time that you are trying to teach your dog. Be patient with yourself; dog training is a physical skill that requires lots of practice and repetition. You will reap the rewards a hundredfold the first time it all comes together and your dog performs perfectly.

FACT

Performing tricks keeps old dogs young, agile, and flexible and gives young energetic dogs an outlet for their energy. There is no truth to the old saying "You can't teach an old dog new tricks." Your elderly companion can indeed pick up new tricks to add to her repertoire.

To teach tricks, you will find you need to be able to break things down into component steps that are easily achieved in a training session. You will get really good at knowing how much information your dog will need to succeed at a given trick, and exactly when to fade out the extra help so that your dog can perform on his own. These skills come with time and practice, but there are several things you can do to help speed up the process:

- Keep a notebook to record your training sessions.
- Before you begin, map out the steps involved in teaching the trick.
- Make sure you make your plan flexible.
- Be ready to add in more detailed steps if your dog has trouble understanding what you want.
- Arm yourself with the best treats and rewards to keep your dog motivated.
- Time your sessions; try not to make them longer than five minutes.
- Read Chapter 4 to familiarize yourself with clicker training; it will save you tons of time in the long run.
- Try to stick to the plan you've mapped out; don't click the dog for lots of different behaviors in one session.

- If you get stuck on one particular trick, brainstorm with a friend about how to help your dog through it.
- Add in distractions as soon as the dog starts to get the hang of what you're trying to teach.
- Don't be afraid to go backward and review previous steps if your dog's behavior falls apart in a new place.

In general, being a good trainer is best indicated by your dog's attitude. If you keep sessions upbeat and fun, make it easy for your dog to succeed, and make sure that you end on a positive note, it won't be long before your dog thinks that working with you is better than anything else in the world.

The Importance of Consistency

Practicing on a regular basis is important if you want to become a good trainer and you want to accomplish the goals you've established for your dog. Designating a time to practice several times a week ensures that you will have lots of opportunities to experiment with techniques, and your dog will have lots of time to get the hang of working with you.

If you have a problem, success will come more easily if you block out specific times during the week and give yourself permission to drop everything for your dog. As you get good at including training in your weekly routine (or daily routine if your dog is young and learning the basics of living politely with humans), you will realize how easy the whole process is. You'll also appreciate how much fun it is to have a dog that works with you because she enjoys it.

Take a Class

Some people find it difficult to block out time for training; they need the consistency of a group class to motivate themselves to practice. Many training schools offer more than obedience classes; some offer agility classes, tricks classes, fly ball, tracking, hunting, herding, or other types of dog sports. Learning something new is more fun when you have the right tools and support, so be sure that the training school's philosophy matches your own and that you feel comfortable there.

Strengthen Your Relationship with Your Dog

When you are training your dog, you are teaching her to share a common language. Teaching your dog the meaning of the basic obedience commands gives you a vocabulary with which to communicate in day-to-day interactions with your dog. As with any communication, you and your dog need to understand each other. Once you find a way that works for you, don't change it. Otherwise, you'll confuse your dog and frustrate yourself.

As you search for the right dog training school, remember that dog training doesn't require the use of force. If you are having problems with your dog's behavior, she needs more training, not heavy-handed corrections and reprimands.

Most people who train their dogs past the basics really begin to appreciate communicating with another species. Specialized training expands your bond with your dog and lets you communicate on a higher level. You will be amazed at just how intelligent dogs are and what can be accomplished through training.

The strong bonds you develop through training will carry over in play and in all the fun things you do with your dog. If your dog likes to swim and you like to walk on the beach, think of how much more enjoyable your time together will be if, when the walk is over, you can simply call your dog and leave.

Fix Behavior Problems

Teaching tricks can help you be more creative about fixing behavior problems with your dog. If you take the time to evaluate why your dog is doing what he is doing, you will figure out a solution that works for you. Some dogs that bark too much are quieter if they are allowed to carry a toy to a visitor. Dogs that jump can learn to do a Bow or Sit and Wave in exchange for petting from guests, or they can do their best version of Roll Over or Play Dead if you need to relax a non–dog person who is afraid of your large dog.

Whatever the problem, use tricks in place of the inappropriate behavior to redirect the dog's energy and enthusiasm. The key here is to make sure that you practice the trick in all different kinds of environments with all different kinds of distractions until your dog's response to the cue is immediate and perfect. The more distraction-proof your tricks are, the more useful they will be to you when you ask the dog to do them.

You will find that dogs with lots of energy are really good at learning tricks. They offer a lot of natural behaviors that are easy to capitalize upon and turn into a trick. Little dogs love to stand on their hind legs or jump in place to see what's on the table, for instance, while big dogs like to spin in circles and stand on their hind legs to take a look out the window or to get your attention.

Teaching your dog simple tricks in one- to three-minute sessions several times a day can help alleviate boredom and create a more content dog. Giving your dog something to think about is a definite furniture saver, but it does not replace common sense about using gates, crates, and pens to keep your dog from getting into trouble in your absence.

Self-Control

Training an energetic dog is fun because they don't tire as easily as other dogs, and they are always willing to try something new. An energetic dog will go along with just about any crazy trick you can dream up; they live for attention any way they can get it. Combining a romp in the park with tricks can give your dog an awesome workout and teach him manners and self-control at the same time.

Most people who own energetic dogs complain at some point about the dog's lack of self-control. Dogs don't just grow out of this; without training they will not one day wake up and behave better. If you don't put the time into training your dog to have better overall manners, you will live with a whirling dervish that never learns to simply hang out with people.

Know the Limits

Performing tricks requires some measure of control on the dog's part because she has to pay attention to your cues and get feedback on what's going right. Dogs that are constantly on the move need skilled trainers who can give them lots of feedback and break the exercise down into tiny steps. Trying to push such dogs too far too fast will result in frustration for both of you. Teaching a dog should be fun regardless of what you train your dog to do. The end result will be a dog that is an enjoyable companion and a treasured member of your family.

Therapy Work

If you need some good reasons to teach your dog lots of goofy tricks, think about the benefits of visiting nursing homes and hospitals. Share your dog's talents with patients who may have owned a dog at some point but no longer have a dog as a part of their daily lives. These folks might really appreciate the warm loving companionship of a well-behaved dog.

If you and your dog are visiting with patients one on one or in a group, use tricks to break the ice and to get people to warm up to your dog. Tricks are a great opening for conversations with patients and you'll often see everyone visibly relax and smile when they see your dog do anything remotely silly. Dogs don't have to do much to make people happy.

Large and dark dogs can sometimes be scary to non–dog people or children. What better way to introduce your dog to someone than to have her do a goofy trick that makes your visitors smile and relax. Play Dead and Roll Over are great for relaxing a guest who does not own a dog.

Trick training is something anyone can do, and getting out there and showing people how much fun it is can be a great way to educate the public about the importance of establishing a relationship with their dogs. Whatever the reason to teach tricks, the bottom line is to have fun with your dog.

CHAPTER 2

What's Your Dog Like?

Taking a moment to get an idea of "who" your dog is can help you design a training program that will be effective in teaching her to fit in with your family. Finding out how your dog responds to distractions and whether she's motivated by toys or games may be helpful in putting together a training program that is easy to implement.

How Well Do You Know Your Dog?

Breaking your training sessions down into small steps, finding out what motivates your dog, and pinpointing where your dog is most distracted will help you know where to start. Ask yourself the following questions before you begin your training program:

- Is your dog energetic or laid back? A maniac retriever or a couch potato?
- Does your dog do something you've always meant to put on cue but didn't know how to?
- Is your dog's attention span short or long? How does he respond amid distractions?
- What is your dog's favorite treat or toy?
- Does your dog give up easily or does he persist until he gets the job done?

Understanding your dog's personality and learning style is essential to enjoyably and successfully teaching him tricks. Combining an energetic dog with a fast moving and flashy trick is exciting and invigorating, both for the dog and for your audience. Knowing your dog means knowing what motivates him. Finding just the right kind of treat, toy, or game for your dog will help him associate training with fun and increase the probability you will succeed.

Energy Level

Some dogs are couch potatoes; others run circles around us all day. Differences in breed, temperament, and personality all come into play when designing a successful training program. Living with your dog makes you the expert when it comes to knowing the ins and outs of her personality and just what will work for her. Paying attention to how active your dog is can help you learn about her personality and help you choose a trick that will be easy and fun to teach.

Highly Active

Active dogs love active tricks because they make the most of natural behaviors, such as spinning, jumping, barking, and pawing. When dogs have this much energy, take advantage of their abilities and teach appropriate tricks.

If you are a beginner and are having a hard time keeping up with your dog, don't be afraid to hire a professional trainer to coach you. The more skills you gain as your dog's trainer, the better you will be able to help your dog understand what you are trying to teach her.

However, high-energy dogs get overstimulated easily and do best in short, concise training sessions with clear goals in mind. If you don't push a high-energy dog to work for long periods, she will fall in love with learning tricks.

Less Active

Lower-energy dogs may be harder to get moving until they figure out what you want them to do. These dogs are thinkers, and they like to know where you're going with all this. Go slowly with your dog. Try to keep your sessions short, because such dogs often bore easily and hate repeating things too many times in a row. Training before a meal (using unique treats as rewards) often perks lower-energy dogs up and lets you get a good session in.

Medium-energy dogs are the easiest to work with because they allow you to make a lot of mistakes and be less organized. They don't mind repeating things over and over, and they are patient with you when you make mistakes or haven't planned out what you are trying to teach. Dogs with moderate energy levels are laid back and fun, turning their energy on like a rocket booster when they need to, but generally going along with whatever you're doing.

Personality

Ask yourself some questions about your dog's personality traits to discover where to begin your training program. It can save a lot of time if you start training your dog in an environment he is comfortable in. An outgoing dog will love tricks that he can perform in a crowd, while a wallflower may prefer performing at a bit of a distance. Teaching your dog where he is most relaxed and least distracted or worried will help him be successful.

Social Temperament

A dog that is easily distracted by his friendliness around people will benefit from training sessions that start somewhere quiet, then quickly move on to involve the distractions he finds hard to resist. Training your dog to perform tricks around distractions from the start is one way to ensure that his performance will not fall apart in public.

Shy dogs, on the other hand, may resist doing tricks in public until they are more confident. With this type of dog, practice in the most comfortable environment possible, and then gradually integrate distractions with familiar people. The ultimate goal is to incorporate strangers and new places so that your dog can perform anywhere.

QUESTION?

How do you work with your dog around distractions?
If you can't get your dog's attention in ten to fifteen seconds, start putting some distance between your dog and the distraction. Increasing the distance will make it easier for your dog to focus and perform the exercise. As he gains confidence and learns to pay attention, you can decrease the distance slowly without losing the behavior.

Special Talents and Interests

A dog will often display a natural talent for certain tricks, depending on his breed. For instance, Labrador and Golden retrievers often excel at tricks that involve having things in their mouths, such as Put away Your Toys or Get

Me a Bottle of Water. Herding breeds might prefer to learn directional tricks, such as spinning to the left or right. A small dog that stands on its hind legs a lot may be a great candidate to learn Dance. A large-breed dog may be perfect for Play Dead, especially if he is of the low-energy mindset.

The most important thing to remember here is that any dog can master tricks that are physically possible for him to do. Dogs are amazing creatures, and they are so willing to be with us and please us that they will put up with a lot so long as they are getting some attention. With enough patience and practice and the right training tools, you can teach your dog to do just about anything!

Keep Safety in Mind

Keep your dog's safety in mind while you are training, and pay attention to her physical limitations. If you have a long-backed breed such as a basset hound for instance, it may not be a good idea to teach her to Sit Up Pretty, since her torso would be awfully heavy to support on such short legs. For larger breeds such as Great Danes and Saint Bernards, you may not want to do any tricks that involve jumping, since the impact of landing is not good for their joints.

FACT

If your dog refuses to assume a certain position, don't be afraid to have her checked for an injury. Dogs are stoic animals and rarely show discomfort unless it's obvious. Hiding injuries is instinctive, stemming from their wolf cousins who live by the rule of survival of the fittest.

Pay attention to your dog's weight, since extra pounds can lead to injuries. If you respect your dog's physical limitations, she will amaze you with her willingness to try what you ask. A dog cannot tell you outright if something is uncomfortable, so do your best to read her body language and go slowly. As often as possible, perform on a soft surface such as a rug, grass, or sand, especially for tricks involving jumping, spinning, or rolling. Being mindful of your environment will minimize injuries and make your dog more comfortable.

What Motivates Your Pooch?

Learning what your dog likes as rewards is crucial to being a successful dog trainer. Many people are surprised to learn that dog cookies and dry dog food just don't cut it. Be creative in what you offer your dog as rewards, and keep the pieces tiny if it's food. Even a Great Dane shouldn't get a treat larger than ¼ inch. Keeping the treats tiny will ensure that you'll be able to train for a longer period of time, because your dog won't fill up too quickly. It will also help ensure that you don't overfeed your dog. Think about cutting his daily ration back a bit if you've had an extra-long training session.

A reward can be anything your dog finds reinforcing.

The reward is your dog's paycheck for playing this training game with you. It has to be something he's willing to work for, not simply something you want him to have. Some people have hang-ups about using food to train dogs because they think it cheapens their bond with the dog. They believe the dog should perform out of respect or love for them. Nonsense. Using food to train your dog is a way to get where you want to go. Training a dog with what he wants as a reward is both respectful to his doggy-ness and effective in the interest of time and resources.

Dogs don't perform out of love; their behavior or misbehavior has nothing to do with their affection for us. Even dogs that chew the couch and bite the mail carrier love their owners. But if you want that biter to like the mail carrier, a pat on the head won't be a strong enough incentive for your dog to do what you want. You'll probably have to use a reward the dog likes a little more.

Dogs are motivated by and will work for food, just like people work for money. We all need money to pay our bills and live our lives; dogs need food to live and enjoy theirs. Many dogs eat out of a bowl once or twice a day for free. Why not take that food and train your dog to behave in a way that is acceptable to you? Once a dog is hooked on training and you have a good bond with him, you can use other rewards to reinforce good or appropriate behavior. Here are some yummy ideas for treats:

- Boiled chicken
- Boiled hamburger
- Popcorn
- Cooked tortellini or other types of pasta
- Bread (bagel pieces work great)
- Carrots
- Bananas
- Dried fruit (not raisins, which can be toxic to dogs)
- Cheerios or other types of cereal
- Freeze-dried liver (found in pet stores and supply catalogs)
- Cooked hot dogs

QUESTION?

How does random reinforcement work?
Once your dog has mastered new tricks and behaviors, start giving him treats sporadically after he obeys a command. He won't know for sure whether he's getting a reward, but he probably won't take the chance of missing one, either.

To prevent your dog from getting diarrhea, don't give him too much of any one thing. As your dog starts to like the training game, mix in less desirable treats (such as dog food) with the yummy stuff so that he never knows what he is getting. Random reinforcement will keep him more interested in the game and let you accomplish more in each training session.

Other Rewards

Most of the time we use a food reward in training because it is quick and easy. Especially in beginner classes, students use treats because there is a lot to accomplish in only one hour a week. If your dog goes nuts over tennis balls or adores chasing Frisbees, use these rewards paired with the click. (See Chapter 4.)

Toys and games are a whole different category of rewards. If you find your dog likes games and toys, make your training sessions even more exciting by mixing them in with food rewards. Some sessions could be all food rewards or all toys and games, or you can mix it up and see what elicits the best response. When you use toys as a reward, the key is to make the play part brief and fun. The game might last five to ten seconds, and then the toy gets hidden and you get back to work. That way the reward doesn't distract the dog from the lesson. Here are some ideas for nonfood rewards:

- A short game of fetch
- A short game of tug
- A short game of catch
- Hide a toy and go find it together
- A toss of a Frisbee
- Chase a stream of bubbles
- Lots of happy praise and baby talk
- Vigorous petting and happy talk
- Flashlight tag (have your dog chase the light beam)
- A stuffed dog toy
- A stuffed dog toy that makes noise
- A squeaky toy with an obnoxious squeaker

Dogs are affectionate animals, and any time you spend praising them and showering them with attention is time well spent. Chances are, you'll get as much from the affection and exercise as they do!

Help Your Dog Like Other Rewards

Some dogs love toys and will happily work for a toss of the ball at least part of the time. Dogs who are not as crazy for toys can learn to like them if you work at it. It is worth the effort on your part to get the dog interested in varied rewards, because the more he finds rewarding the easier it will be for you and the more effective your sessions will be. Here's how to get started:

1. Hold your dog on a leash and tease him with a toy.
2. Throw the toy out of range and ignore his struggle toward it, but don't let him get it.
3. Use a helper to make the toy more exciting if necessary.
4. Wait patiently until the dog looks away from the toy and back at you.
5. Mark that moment with a click and allow him to go play with the toy as the reward (see Chapter 4).
6. If your dog doesn't turn away from the toy in about thirty seconds, slowly back up to increase the distance between the dog and the toy. When your dog looks back at you, click and release him to get the toy.
7. Repeat this with different toys and allow the dog to go play with the helper every once in a while.
8. The play part of the reward should be brief, about ten seconds.

This exercise should help you rev up a dog that is only mildly interested in toys. Warming him up this way is often a great way to start a training session because it helps the dog realize that it's time to work.

Exciting rewards are critical to an effective program. If your dog isn't turning himself inside out for the reward, find something he likes better. Don't worry if you just can't get your dog interested in toys; there is no crime in using food in training. Remember that your dog normally eats for free every day, so it's okay to make him work for it instead.

Reward or Bribe?

Using food to teach your dog to perform tricks is simple, fun, and effective. However, many people complain that the dog won't perform the behavior in the absence of food. That just means you aren't there yet. If you use food correctly, you won't need to use it to get the dog to perform the trick; it will come after the trick has been performed. This is the critical difference between a reward and a bribe.

A bribe is something that causes a behavior to happen by enticing the dog. For example, your dog is out in the yard and won't come in, so you shake a box of cookies to bribe him in. This isn't really a bad thing, but it isn't training either. Bribing can have its benefits when you are in a hurry and out of options.

FACT

Be mindful of the difference between bribes and rewards; they can mean the difference between a well-managed dog whose behavior is dependent upon your attentiveness and her hunger level, and the well-*trained* dog who responds to cues immediately and reliably because she knows the consequences will be good.

A reward, on the other hand, is something that occurs only after a behavior happens. A reward reinforces the likelihood that the behavior will happen again. For instance, you call your dog at the park and he comes to you; you offer a treat and release him back to play again. A rewarded dog is far more likely to come to you the next time you call than is a dog that is put back on leash and put in the car to go home. Two types of rewards are at work here: the food reward, which reinforced the dog for performing the behavior of coming back to his owner; and the consequence for coming back, which was that he got to go play again.

If you know your dog well—his energy level, personality, special talents, limitations, and motivations—you will be able to choose tricks that make both of you shine. Spend some time with your dog over the next few days and make notes on each of these categories. You may be surprised to learn how many things you assumed he would like that he actually doesn't. Adjusting your teaching style and training sessions can have a profound impact on the success of your training program.

CHAPTER 3

Give Your Dog a Job

Most animals have a basic need for food, water, and shelter, which we provide for our dogs with barely a second thought. However, we often overlook exercise and mental stimulation, and greater attention in these areas can mean the difference between a really great dog and a problem dog.

Exercise First; Training Will Follow

Exercise is a crucial element in any training program. Without enough of it, no real learning will occur. A dog without enough exercise is like a child without recess. What adult would like to teach a math lesson to a classroom full of six-year-olds who haven't been outside to play all day? Without exercise, your dog will be hard to teach because she just can't be still long enough to pay attention.

Dogs vary in their exercise requirements, but all need at least thirty minutes of running, playing, and interaction with you each day. The amount and type of exercise is dependent upon your dog's overall energy level. A Border collie or active young Lab will need one to two hours of flat-out running and active play, while a couch potato Pekingese may need only a thirty-minute romp. Yet, every dog is different, regardless of the breed and its stereotype. Ultimately, the amount of exercise your dog needs is whatever it takes to make her tired enough to be able to exist in your home as a calm, relaxed member of the family. The following clues will help you recognize if your dog isn't getting enough exercise:

- She paces from room to room in the house.
- She hardly ever lies down, even when everyone else is relaxed.
- She whines excessively for no apparent reason.
- She barks excessively, sometimes over nothing.
- She digs, destroys, and chews everything in sight.
- She never stops jumping when there are people around.
- She runs away every chance she gets.
- She runs along the fence, using any excuse to bark at passersby.

If your dog exhibits some or all of these symptoms, she could probably use more exercise and mental stimulation. Most people don't realize that leaving their dogs in the backyard for hours at a time is not a good way to burn off energy. Your dog doesn't get nearly enough exercise to make for a relaxed family pet. Most dogs, when left to their own devices, don't do anything but bark, dig, or lie around.

If you are going to use your yard as a way to exercise your dog, you will need to go out with her and play games to burn off even a fraction of the energy she's got bottled up. Inviting neighbor dogs over to play might be another option as long as the dogs get along with each other. All-out running, chasing, and wrestling is what a dog needs to do to be tired enough to be a good pet.

FACT

Energetic dogs that don't get enough exercise are obvious; they exhibit their excess energy in excessive barking, jumping, and other unwanted behavior. If your dog has behavior problems, increasing the amount of exercise she gets can cut your training time in half.

Work Out Together

For dog owners with an active lifestyle, there are lots of ways a healthy active dog can burn off energy with you. Jogging, mountain biking, and Rollerblading are excellent ways to exercise dogs with boundless energy. Just make sure that you start off slowly and gradually build the distance. Also, pay attention to your dog's feet, checking them frequently for cuts and scrapes. Try to have him run on a variety of surfaces, since pavement is hard on a dog's joints and bones.

Dogs that participate in such activities should be at least one year old and recently checked by their veterinarians for potential health problems. (Just as it can with people, vigorous exercise can exacerbate certain bone and joint disorders.) A fit dog is happier, and you will find that he is more focused on whatever activity you are enjoying together, and he will be more likely to do it longer and without injury.

Dog Sports and Activities

The reason many people get dogs in the first place is to enjoy their company and share them with other people. Depending on your dog's personality and activity level, you may consider participating with your dog in any of a great variety of dog sports or activities. Enrolling your dog in an agility class might be an excellent way to introduce both of you to something new while maintaining a good level of fitness. Agility is an obstacle course for dogs, usually comprised of hurdles to jump over and things to climb over, around, and through. The course is timed, and your success depends on your ability to lead your dog through a maze of obstacles to the finish.

A golden retriever competes in an agility trail.

If you would like to be an active participant in your dog's exercise program, you will find that many canine sports require you to be almost as fit as your dog. From fly ball to tracking to search and rescue, the possibilities are endless. If your style is quieter, you may consider a visiting-therapy dog program that allows you to go and visit a hospital or nursing home on a weekly or monthly basis. This is an excellent way to meet other dog owners and keep your dog's obedience skills sharp, because you will use them constantly.

If you have a lot of free time and financial resources, you may consider becoming part of the growing number of search and rescue dog teams that look for missing people locally and nationally. No matter what your interest, there is a dog sport out there that you and your pup will both enjoy.

Games Dogs Play

Games are a great way to simultaneously boost your dog's interest in learning new things and strengthen your bond with him. Regardless of the game, the true objective is to make sure you both have fun. Keep the rules simple and easy to follow, and play often. Involve as many people in the family as you can, and see how much fun it can be to learn new ways of interacting together. Consider any of the following activities and games:

- **Play fetch:** This is a great way to tire out a tireless retriever. Use a tennis racquet to hit the ball that much further for all-out sprints.
- **Go swimming:** Here's another great way to exercise a very active dog. Combine it with some retrieving for a really exhausting workout.
- **Play hide-and-seek:** This indoor rainy-day game may provide some dogs with enough activity to let them sleep the rest of the day. Also use this game to perk up your dog's recall and teach him that coming to you is always the best option.
- **Hide your dog's toys:** He'll learn to use his nose to track things down *and* bring them back to you.
- **Learn a new trick:** Practice until it's perfect, then show off to your friends and family.
- **Practice Pavlov:** Set up a treat-dispensing toy and show your dog how to interact with it until it pays off.

Whatever you do, be sure you have a blast! Keep it fun, and keep the pace fast and interesting; you will see your dog perk up at the mere mention of playtime with you.

In this dog-friendly age of ours, services like doggie day care, play groups, and dog parks are available to help us exercise our restless pooches. If you try to fit in more exercise sessions but just can't seem to put a dent in your dog's energy, consider doggie day care one or two days a week.

Provide the Right Foundation for Learning

Mental stimulation is the second most overlooked need of problem dogs. Learning new things and solving problems make life interesting and give smart dogs something to do, and it keeps them out of trouble! All dogs, regardless of breed or energy level, are intelligent and interactive creatures that love new experiences.

Dogs that are tied outside, constantly frustrated and emotionally neglected, may start off friendly and welcoming but eventually become aggressive and wary of strangers. They have nothing to do, nothing to think about, and are absolutely bored. Dogs like this, even early in their adult lives (two to three years old), are hard to train. They aren't stupid or uncooperative, just blank. They simply do not know how to learn.

Lack of early stimulation and training makes it more difficult to teach any animal at a later date, because a dog has no basis for and doesn't quite know what to make out of the attention. It is possible to teach these dogs, but it takes patience, repetition, and practice. The training methods and tools described in the succeeding chapters will help you teach your dog anything you care to take the time to teach her.

Teach Your Dog to Think

The training methods described in this book teach your dog how to think and solve problems, which is important for any dog. The techniques are commonly referred to as "clicker training," and they are based in proven scientific theory. The rules and guidelines (see Chapter 4) will show you how to use this method to teach your dog anything physically possible. It is exciting to see a dog grasp the concept of what you are trying to accomplish and to watch her respond without needing any corrections!

FACT

As you read and do research, you will find that there is no one way to train a dog. As your dog's primary caretaker, it is your job to find the methods that get the job done without harming your relationship. Find a trainer who emphasizes building your relationship with your dog.

All puppies should attend a well-run puppy kindergarten class that instructs you how to teach your dog the basic commands—Sit, Down, Stay, Come—how to walk without pulling, and to come when called. The class should also offer a playtime for dogs in the eight- to eighteen-week range and should be staff-supervised so everyone has a good experience. It is crucial to the normal social development of your dog that she gets to play with other puppies and safe, well-socialized adult dogs on a regular basis. The more good experiences your young puppy has, the easier it will be to teach her anything later in life.

Look for the following qualities when you search for a dog-training school:

- A limited class size with an instructor/assistant-to-student ratio of 1:6 is ideal.
- The age of the puppies accepted should be no older than eighteen weeks.
- Handouts or homework sheets to explain exercises are important so that lessons can be shared among family members.
- The whole family should be welcome to attend. (If you include your children, make sure there are at least two adults so one can supervise the kids while the other focuses on training the dog.)
- All training methods should be positively based; ideally clicker training.
- Demonstrations should be given with untrained dogs to show the progression of exercises.
- Volunteers or assistants who help with the management of the class should be available to ensure that you get the help you need.

If a method makes you uncomfortable, don't do it. If you're not sure if something will work but the technique won't do any harm, go ahead and try it so you can see for yourself. Your dog will benefit greatly from an owner who is committed to finding the best way possible to train her to be the best companion she can be.

The best judge of a good puppy kindergarten—or any obedience class for that matter—is you. Ask if you can observe a class before signing up. Make sure the methods taught are kind and gentle and that the puppies seem to be getting it. Go on your gut instinct. If you like the instructor and she seems like a person you can learn from, sign up. Train your dog; it's the nicest way to say you love her!

Practice and Consistency Are Key

As with anything in which you want to excel, the more you practice, the better at it you will become. All training is a learned skill; the more you work with your dog, the more effective you'll be as a trainer and as a team. For example, the beginning trainer is notoriously stingy with rewards, and her timing needs some work. Through lots of practice, you will find and develop your own training style, discovering what works for you and expanding upon it.

You can find tons of resources—books, videos, and Internet sites—that will tell you everything you'll ever want to know about behavior and training. Search for obedience classes in your area and keep at it. Remember that you and your dog are going to be together for a very long time—maybe even ten to twelve years or longer. You will both benefit from the time you spend teaching her how to learn. Start your dog on the road to higher learning today!

CHAPTER 4

Clicker Training

In recent years, dog training has become kinder and gentler to both the dog and the owner. No longer is it necessary to use brute force or intimidation to force a dog to comply. Training any animal is about opening lines of communication and learning a common language. Clicker training isn't a gimmick or the latest fad; it is a technique that is based in science. It uses the positive principles of operant conditioning (training your dog to offer the desired behavior before she receives a reward).

The Kindness Revolution in Dog Training

Use clicker training to teach your dog what you expect of him; it's an intelligent and overall time-saving endeavor. Positive reinforcement through the use of treats and a clicker will help you teach your dog to think. The old style of training—making the dog "obey"—is not only outdated, it does not evolve his problem-solving skills or intelligence.

Training your dog with treats and a clicker is the fastest, most reliable way to train your dog and have fun while you are doing it. There is no need to coerce, push, or shove to get what you want; once your dog knows how to learn, you will have a willing partner and a better overall relationship. Hundreds of families have learned to train their dogs with clickers and treats, and they found the learning process so enjoyable that they have come back again and again for more advanced classes.

FACT

Animals in zoos, aquariums, and circuses have been trained operantly using positive reinforcement for decades. Can you picture putting a training collar on a killer whale and trying to make it jump? Just because you can force dogs to obey doesn't mean you should. Teach your dog to think instead!

The application of clicker training to dogs is pure genius; it simplifies and speeds up the process of learning for dogs and owners alike. Handlers of any age or size can learn the principles of clicker training, and since it is not dependent on corrections or physical manipulation, the size, strength, and stamina of the handler doesn't matter.

Getting Started with a Clicker

A clicker is a small, plastic box with a metal tab that makes a clicking sound when you push down with your thumb. The sound of the click is paired with a food reward by clicking the clicker and giving the dog a treat. After a few repetitions, the dog learns to associate the sound of the clicker with a food reward.

Why It Works

The click marks the desired behavior to help the dog identify which behavior earned the reward. Because the food is removed by a step—you click first and then treat—you will find that your dog will work for the sound of the click rather than just a food reward. Pairing the clicker with a food reward creates a powerful way to tell your dogs which behaviors are rewardable. This comes in handy, especially with a very active dog, because it gives you a way to specify to the dog exactly which of the behaviors earned the reward.

Starting with food rewards is faster than using toys and games. Once the dog begins to understand clicker training and how the game works, you can use other rewards, including balls, tug toys, or playtime with other dogs.

Think of the click as a snapshot of what the dog is doing at a particular moment. The click clearly identifies for the dog which behavior is being rewarded. Not only does this make it easier for the dog to understand what she is doing right, but it also gets her excited about the learning process since it gives her the responsibility of making the click happen.

The Clicker As an Event Marker

The sound of the click is unique, like nothing the dog has ever heard, which is part of the key to its success in shaping behavior. People often ask about using their voices instead of a clicker to mark the behavior they are looking for. In the initial stages of training, your voice is not a good event marker because you talk to your dog all the time, so your voice lacks the startling effect of a clicker. A clicker's uniqueness reaches the part of the brain that is also responsible for the fight-or-flight response. In short, it really captures the dog's attention.

The process of shaping is what clicker training is all about. Shaping is useful in all types of training, but it is crucial in teaching tricks. Shaping behavior helps the dog learn how to think about what she did to earn the reward. By not helping her or physically manipulating her body, you help your dog learn faster and more permanently by trial and error. Clicking, or its absence, indicates which behaviors will be rewarded and which will not.

Once the dog has the idea that a treat follows each click, remove the treats from your person and put them on a table, chair, or step. The dog will still get the treat after being clicked for the right behavior, but the treat will no longer be in your hand or pocket. This exercise will teach your dog to pay attention to the click, not the presence of the treat.

Shaping

Shaping behavior means breaking it down into steps that progress toward an end goal. Shaping is not a rigid list of steps, but rather a general guide to get from point A to point B with lots of room for variation, intuition, rapid progress, or reviewing.

Prompted and Free Shaping

Shaping can be either prompted, using a food lure or target, or free shaped. Free shaping requires waiting for the dog to offer desired actions on his own, then rewarding him with a treat to capture the small steps of behavior that lead toward the end goal. Each trick you learn here will be broken down into its component parts. You can then embellish upon those steps if your dog needs things broken down further. Free shaping is definitely worth adding to your bag of tricks. It gives you one more way to explain what you want your dog to do. You just show up with your clicker and treats, and you click and treat what you like and ignore what you don't.

Keep notes on each trick you teach. Write down whether your dog is catching on to the components as presented or if he needs more explicit direction. You will find that detailed notes make it easy to pick up where you left off, and your training sessions will be more productive overall. You will reach your goals faster if you have a plan.

FACT

Training a behavior is not always a process that moves in one direction. Don't ever be afraid to quit a training session and go back to it later with a better plan and a fresh mind. Sometimes the best way to move forward is to take a rest.

For behaviors that involve natural talents or unusual behaviors, free shaping is the way to go. Because the dog is fully in charge of which behaviors he is offering, he will often learn faster and retain more than when you prompt his behavior with a lure or target. However, free shaping can be time consuming since it depends upon the dog offering the behavior, and it requires patience on the handler's part.

Working Through a Shaping Plan

Teaching a dog that likes to jump on guests to Sit instead is a lot more complicated than teaching just a Sit/Stay. This is because of the sheer number of potential distractions and variables during any given greeting. Though a dog may be able to Sit when there are no distractions, this doesn't mean he'll be able to Sit when a kid with a hot dog approaches him or when he sees his favorite person. Dogs need to be taught how to Sit and Stay around gradually more stimulating distractions; they don't automatically generalize their behavior to all environments.

Teaching your dog to Sit instead of jumping requires that you break sitting down into small steps that are easy for the dog to accomplish. Introduce challenging distractions slowly so as to maintain the right behavior. The steps to teach Sit/Stay around distractions are as follows:

1. Teach your dog to Sit by luring him with a treat, then clicking and treating him when his bottom hits the floor.
2. Once your dog is performing this well, delay the click by counting to two before you click and treat. This is the beginning of a mini-Stay.

3. Increase the amount of seconds between the time your dog sits and the click and treat until your dog is holding the Sit behavior for ten seconds at a time.

4. Once your dog can hold the Sit for ten seconds between clicks and treats, go ahead and verbally label the behavior Stay and include a hand signal if desired.

5. Help your dog generalize this behavior by going somewhere new or adding in distractions. You may have to lower your standards and start from the beginning until your dog learns to block out the distractions and pay attention to you instead.

6. Add in people approaching your dog from the side and not making eye contact.

7. Add in people approaching your dog from the front and looking at him.

8. Add in people petting him or talking to him.

9. Continue to change the variables until your dog will hold the Sit/Stay position regardless of the distraction.

10. As your dog starts to be able to handle the distractions and works longer and more consistently, wean him off the clicker and treats so that he will perform the behavior for the reward of being able to greet the person.

ALERT!

Dogs are not good at generalizing their behavior; they don't automatically transfer it to other surroundings. A dog who will Sit in the kitchen on the first try may never Sit at the pet store or the park. If you want to have control over your dog's behavior anywhere, you have to train everywhere.

Using this shaping plan, you can teach your dog to sit regardless of what is happening in the environment or who he is greeting. The following steps detail a less formal way to teach the same thing. You might try both shaping plans to see which one is more suited to your training style. The following shaping plan does not help the dog by luring him with a treat when he makes the wrong decision. Instead, this shaping sequence lets the dog make choices. You click only those choices that lead toward the goal of sitting and staying.

ALERT!

The dog will often revert back to old habits like jumping and whining. Simply ignore the things you don't want. The dog will soon realize that those behaviors are not rewardable and will start paying attention to only the behaviors he is being clicked for.

1. Start off by clicking and treating the dog for any behavior except jumping (standing, sitting, lying down, walking around) for the first minute.
2. The second minute choose something specific and click and treat him every time he offers it. You'll want to pick something easy, like standing still for one second or walking without whining, so that he can easily succeed.
3. If you have an active dog that offers a lot of behaviors, you might want to limit his options by putting him on a leash and stepping on it so that jumping is not an option.
4. Continue working with the dog in short sessions until he starts to visibly startle at the sound of the click and holds the position for a second.
5. Next, withhold the click for a while and see what happens; most dogs will Sit out of confusion and boredom, and you can click and treat that.
6. As soon as the dog Sits (on his own without being prompted), click and treat.
7. Repeat this over and over and gradually increase the amount of seconds the dog has to hold the Sit for a click and treat, until you have the dog holding the Sit for a reasonable amount of time (about 10 seconds).
8. You can continue to polish the Sit to greet visitors in any way you wish.

Regardless of which shaping plan you choose, you will see that there are times when things will go quickly and smoothly, and you may even skip steps or make great leaps in your shaping plan. Other times you will come to a standstill as your dog gets muddled and confused about what he's supposed to do. You will need to re-evaluate your plan and break it down into further steps or help him out in some way. Learning how to shape behavior will make you a better overall dog trainer, and training your dog will be more fun.

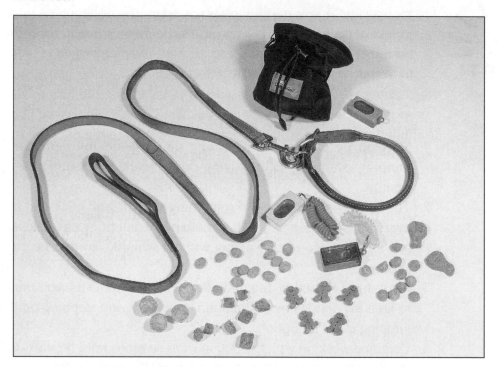

Tools of the trade: bait bag, flat collar, leash, clicker, and bite-sized treats.

Using Lures in Training

A lure is a piece of food that is used to elicit behavior. Its goal is to help the dog get into the right position to earn the click and treat. In beginning your career as a dog trainer, it is often frustrating and time consuming to wait for your dog to offer the right behavior. The use of a food lure gets things going. The problem with food lures is that unless they are faded relatively quickly, the dog (and humans) become dependent upon them to perform the behavior. If lures are not faded, you will not have a trained dog that can perform behaviors on cue; you will have a trained dog that follows food.

As a general rule, lure the dog six times in a row. On the seventh repetition, do all the same motions with your body, but without the food lure in your hand. If the dog performs the behavior correctly, click and treat. If she doesn't perform the behavior correctly, go back and lure her six more times and try it again. This mini-drilling session trains the dog on how to perform the correct behavior, and it lets you see if she understands what she's being clicked for.

Your goal with using a food lure is to help the dog into position six times in a row. On the seventh repetition, try hiding the lure to see if the dog starts to offer the behavior on her own. When you take the lure out of your hand, you can start fading it gradually by putting it on a nearby table and running to get it after the click. The dog knows it's there and is excited about it but is not dependent on you waving it around to get her into the right position.

Using this method to wean your dog off of lures means that you get the dog to perform the behavior, click, and then run to get the treat. Doing this exercise will help your dog to learn that she is working for the click and the treat is an afterthought.

QUESTION?

Do all dogs respond to lures?
For some dogs, lures present more of a distraction and a hindrance than a help. For such dogs, you should skip the lure altogether.

Targeting

Targeting is a form of luring, but it removes the treat by a step. It involves teaching the dog to touch his nose to an object. You might use this tool to move your dog or have him interact with someone or something. Anything can be used as a target, but the three main targets are your hand, the lid to a yogurt container, and a target stick. (You can buy a target stick online at *www.clickertraining.com* or make your own out of a short piece of dowel.)

Hand Target

The goal with using targeting is to get the behavior started and then wean the dog off the target so that he is performing the behavior reliably without it. The same rules apply to weaning off the target as with weaning off the lure. Use it to get the behavior started and then wean your dog off of it. To teach your dog to target your hand with his nose, follow these steps:

1. Hold your hand palm-up with a piece of food tucked under your thumb in the center of your palm. Click and treat your dog for sniffing your hand.
2. Keep the food in your hand for six repetitions and then take the food out and repeat, clicking the dog for touching his nose to your palm.
3. Have the dog follow your hand in all directions while you move around the room.
4. Involve a helper and have your dog target your hand and then your helper's hand for clicks and treats.
5. Label the behavior of touching his nose to your hand by saying Touch.
6. Try the trick in new places and with new people until your dog is fluent. Don't be afraid to go back to using food for a few repetitions if your dog falls apart around a new distraction.

Lid Target

On occasion, you may want your dog to move away from you to perform a behavior at a distance. In that case, it may be useful for you to teach your dog to target a yogurt lid with his nose. The steps for teaching your dog to target a lid are:

1. Put the lid in your hand and hold a treat in the center with your thumb.
2. When your dog noses at it, click and treat. Repeat for six repetitions.
3. Present the lid with no treat and click and treat for sniffing or nose bumping.
4. Label the behavior by saying Touch again just before your dog touches the lid.

5. Put the lid on the floor close by and repeat, clicking your dog at first for moving toward the lid and then for actually touching it with his nose.

6. Move the lid at varying distances until you can send him across the room to bump it with his nose for a click and treat.

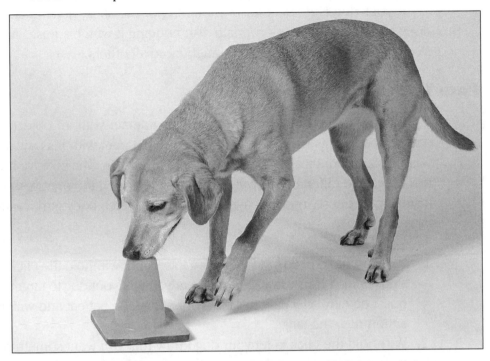

Targeting an object can be used to increase confidence and help a scared dog move from one place to another—the car, the bathtub, etc.

Stick Target

Another variation of targeting involves using a stick as your target. The target stick acts like an extension of your arm and is useful in working with your dog at a little distance from you. The steps for teaching your dog to touch a target stick with his nose are as follows:

1. Put the end of the stick in the palm of your hand with a treat and click and treat your dog for sniffing or nudging at it with his nose.

2. Gradually work your hand up the stick and only click and treat your dog for touching his nose close to the end away from your hand.

3. Try putting the stick on the floor and only clicking and treating when your dog touches the ends.

4. Have your dog follow the stick as you walk with him until he's racing to catch the end of it for a click and treat.

If your dog is doing a lot of mouthing of the stick, don't click until he does something more appropriate, like nudging it with his nose. Be careful to click only appropriate touches and ignore all others.

Paw Targeting

Sometimes you may want your dog to interact with an object with his paw instead of his nose. Teaching your dog to target with his paw may give you another tool that you can use to help him learn whatever trick you are teaching. The difference between teaching your dog to target with his paw instead of his nose involves paying attention to which body part is hitting the target.

1. Put your hand or lid out for the dog to see, but withhold the click until he steps near it. Because you have already taught your dog to target with his nose, he may offer only this behavior at first. Be patient and wait for paw action near the target.

2. Withhold the click to let your dog know that you want something other than a nose touch and see what happens.

3. Make it easy on your dog by moving the lid or your hand along the floor so that you can click him for moving toward it. An easy way to help your dog to get this behavior started is to put the lid at the base of the stairs and click him for stepping on or next to it.

4. When you withhold the click, your dog may get frustrated, but don't be too quick to help right away; wait your dog out and see if he'll paw at the target or move toward it.

5. Practice a paw target separately from a nose target and be sure to have two distinctive cues for each one.

6. Short, frequent training sessions will help your dog figure out what you want faster than long, confusing ones.

For targeting to be useful, you must practice it often. The more experience your dog has with this method, the better it will serve you in your trick training.

Teaching the dog to touch his paw to a hand target can be the starting point for teaching many other fun and useful behaviors.

Labeling Behavior

The major difference between clicker training and other types of training is that you don't label the behavior right away. The reason for this is that the early versions of the behavior are not what you want for the final behavior. The first click for heeling, for instance, is a far cry from what the finished behavior will be. Saving the label until the dog is readily offering the behavior will ensure that the dog connects its behavior with what is being clicked, first.

The label can come as a verbal cue or a hand signal or both, but it should not be introduced until the dog is offering a decent version of it. If you label behavior too soon, you will get a wide variety of responses from the dog. Wait until the behavior looks close to perfect before labeling it.

You can call each behavior anything you want, but try to label each behavior as a simple one-syllable word as often as possible. Try to be sure it doesn't sound too much like any other word you use with your dog. Dogs pick up a lot from your body language and the pitch of your voice but may have trouble distinguishing between similar sounding words, like *no* and *go* for instance.

FACT

Asking your dog to perform a behavior assumes that she knows what the label or cue means. Follow the Ten in a Row rule before asking for a particular behavior. The dog should perform the behavior (without clicking, treating, or luring) ten times in a row without any mistakes. If she doesn't have 100 percent accuracy, do more training.

Weaning off the Clicker and Treats

The clicker is a learning tool, a signal that identifies for the dog which behaviors will be rewarded. When the dog is performing the behavior on cue and reliably (with 100 percent accuracy), he is ready to be weaned off the clicker and treats. The click and treat always go together. You shouldn't click without treating because the value of the reward marker, the click, will become diluted and less meaningful to the dog.

How to Phase Out Clicking and Treating

One way to begin the weaning process is to have the dog repeat the behavior more than once before you click and treat. This gives the dog the idea that he must continue to perform the behavior until he hears his click. The worst thing you can do when you are weaning your dog off the clicker and treats is to do it cold turkey. Getting rid of rewards and affirmation all at once is too abrupt, and it will result in a frustrated dog.

The key to weaning is going slowly, getting the dog to perform longer versions of the behavior, or successfully performing it in more repetitions. The weaning process may be a good time to start introducing nonfood rewards, such as the opportunity to go greet a guest after sitting, or being released to go play with other dogs after coming when called.

The Last Word on Using Food

Eating is most dogs' greatest joy, a pleasure that you can use to help your dog learn appropriate manners and become a well-behaved member of your family. Regardless of a dog's preference for particular types of food, all dogs need to eat to survive. Whether your dog is food oriented or not, every dog will work for food. You just may need to search a bit to find the right kind. What instructors love about clicker training is that it works for every dog.

Don't use fattening dog biscuits as treats. When it comes to calories, one dog cookie is like eating a snack-size candy bar. Instead, use things like carrot sticks or soft dog treats cut into small pieces.

Clicker training is successful because the emphasis is on the click, not the treat. Once dogs figure out the game, they love it and will gladly work regardless of how they feel about food. If you have a finicky fellow, try diversifying what you use as the reward and cutting back a little on his daily meal.

For dogs that like to eat, you may have the opposite problem: too many calories. Clicker training uses a lot of food rewards, but that doesn't mean you'll have a fat dog. The size of the rewards should be tiny—¼ of an inch or less—and can even consist of the dog's meals. If you have a particularly long training session, you can feed less food at the next meal or actually use the meal to train. The length of your sessions should be five to ten minutes maximum, so your dog is not going to be getting a lot of extra treats at one time. If your dog is on a special diet, consult your veterinarian and find out what food treats you can use.

The beauty of clicker training is that it teaches dogs to think. It is a kind, nonviolent way to teach a dog what is expected of her. It is also long lasting and easy, making it fun for the trainer and trainee alike. Enjoy using this method to teach your dog anything your heart desires, starting with some of the coolest tricks around!

CHAPTER 5

Dog Training Basics

The time you spend training your dog is critical to developing and fostering a relationship with her. Training in itself is a relationship because of the way you communicate with your dog and develop a common language of words and signals. Dogs that are trained to respond to basic commands are more fun to own because you can direct their behavior for a more enjoyable life together.

Invest in the Future

An untrained dog still learns things, just not necessarily the things you want him to know. Part of your dog's training and communication skills has to do with the structure you provide for him. You must tell him what is and is not allowed. Putting in the time to teach your dog the basics around various distractions and in new environments is part of being a good dog owner, and it will help you avoid future behavior problems. The better trained your dog is, the better your relationship with one another.

Leadership Involves Controlling Resources

Dogs are pack animals; they thrive on rules, consistency, and expectations. Setting limits about what is allowed and how you expect them to act is not only fair, but also essential to having a healthy, well-adjusted dog. Don't worry! Being a strong, fair leader is not about being physical with your dog. A true leader would never need to pin a dog down or give a harsh correction.

Leadership isn't about forcing dogs to obey. It requires you to provide structure and establish boundaries by controlling resources. The more time you spend establishing that you are the greatest person in your dog's life, the more control you will have over your dog's behavior. If your dog understands that you are the one who has the ability to give him access to everything that is important to him, he will be better behaved.

Leadership is about controlling access to the things your dog wants, including sleeping and resting places, food, toys, attention, access to other dogs, and access to the outdoors. It is about *you* being in command, not the dog.

The relationship between a well-behaved dog and his owner is one that consists of limits and rules about what is expected, as well as consistent training so the dog can recognize what is expected. Developing a relationship through training will mean that you will always have a way to communicate with your dog, and you will be able to nip behavior problems in the bud or avoid them all together. Being a strong leader is the first step toward ridding your dog of behavior problems. The following are some guidelines on how to be a strong, fair leader:

1. Nothing in life is free. Make sure you give your dog a job. Make him Sit for dinner, Lie Down before doors are opened for him, and so on.

2. Humans go first through doorways and up and down the stairs. Your dog won't be able to escape out the door or knock you over on your way down the stairs if he is always behind you. Teach your dog to Sit and Stay until he is released through the door.

3. Down/Stay sessions for five to twenty minutes at a time help teach your dog self-control and give him a constructive job to perform around distractions and company.

4. No dogs are allowed on the beds or furniture. Young dogs should sleep in a crate or in their own beds, not in bed with you. Your bed is the highest, most special place in the house, and it should be reserved for you only.

5. Don't repeat a command more than once. If your dog doesn't respond on the first try, he does not get what you were offering.

6. Follow through. If you've asked your dog to do something but he does not respond, make sure you help him to get into the right position rather than repeating the command.

7. Ignore your dog if he nudges you for attention. Leaders give attention on their own terms, not when their dogs demand it.

8. Ignore your dog if he is constantly pushing toys at you. Leaders initiate play and decide when the game starts and ends. This keeps a dog on his toes because he never knows when the fun begins.

9. Provide consequences. Ignore what you don't like; avoid yelling at your dog for barking or jumping, for instance. From your dog's perspective, any attention is better than none, and speaking to the dog can often be mistaken for reinforcement.

10. Avoid punishment. Instead, teach your dog what you want him to do.

Because you control the things your dog wants access to, your leadership will help you build a strong bond with your dog, convincing him that you are the key to everything he desires. Strong leadership will give you the foundation you need to teach your dog how to behave appropriately and become a welcomed member of the family.

The Ten Keys to Successful Training

Throughout this book, you will learn effective techniques to ensure the success of you as a trainer, and your dog as a student. Most keys to success are universal, but it will be helpful for you to think of them in terms of your pet.

1. **Be patient.** All dogs learn at different speeds and often don't grasp concepts as quickly as we think they should. Be patient with your dog and help him to be successful.
2. **Plan ahead.** Set your dog up to succeed. If your dog isn't getting it, the behavior probably needs to be broken down into smaller steps.
3. **Be realistic.** Don't expect your dog to perform a behavior in an environment you haven't taught him in.
4. **Be kind.** Use positive methods to teach your dog what's expected of him.
5. **Avoid punishment.** Harsh corrections have no place in the learning phase of a dog's development.
6. **Reward effectively.** Reinforce proper behavior with what motivates your dog. A pat on the head is nice but not necessarily what he wants. Remember that this is his paycheck: Pay up!
7. **Be generous.** New trainers tend to be cheap with rewards. Reward correct responses often and don't be afraid to reward exceptionally good responses with extra treats, praise, toys, and love.
8. **Set goals.** If you don't know where you are going and have not planned out the session, how will you know when your dog's got it?
9. **Practice often.** Teach your dog in short frequent sessions.
10. **Stay positive.** Quit while you're ahead, when your dog is still excited about the training and wants to do more. An enthusiastic student is always an eager learner.

The simple truth of training dogs is that you get what you pay attention to. Set your dog up to succeed, limit his options, and reinforce what's going right. Soon you'll have a well-behaved dog that everyone loves to have around.

Teaching the Basics

Basic obedience is part of most tricks. The better your dog responds to commands like Sit/Stay and Down/Stay, the easier it will be to teach any trick, especially the more complicated ones. The basics of Sit, Down, Stay, and Come are the foundation for most of the tricks that are covered in this book. If nothing else, having some knowledge of the basics will help your dog relax enough to learn something new. Teaching your dog how to sit or lie down can help you position her for success. You can't just expect that working with your dog for a session or two will make her reliable around distractions and new people. If you want your dog to be well behaved and respond to your commands consistently, you must put in the time to train her.

Teaching Sit

Teaching Sit involves luring the dog into position before you click and treat for the correct response. Remember that when using a lure, it's important to fade its presence quickly to keep the dog from becoming dependent upon it. Fading a lure is an important part of making sure your dog becomes reliable and is truly grasping the concept of sitting. The steps to teaching Sit are as follows:

1. Hold a treat slightly above your dog's nose and bring it back slowly over her head.
2. When your dog's bottom hits the ground, click and treat.
3. If your dog keeps backing up, practice against a wall so she can only go so far.
4. Repeat this until your dog is offering Sit readily.
5. Take the treat out of your hand and, holding your hand the same way, entice your dog to Sit. If she Sits, click and treat; if she doesn't, go back to using a food lure for six to eight more repetitions.

6. Once your dog is doing this reliably (follow the Ten in a Row rule), verbally label the behavior Sit right before the dog's bottom hits the ground.

7. Repeat these steps in various places until your dog is responding well with no mistakes.

8. Now, without a treat in your hand, ask your dog to repeat the behavior more than once before you click and treat. Start with low numbers of repetitions like two, three, or four Sits before you click and treat, but don't follow a pattern.

9. To help her generalize the behavior, start practicing somewhere new— the pet store, the park, the vet's office. Remember that forgetting is a normal part of learning and you will need to go back to helping the dog, with a treat in your hand if necessary, if the place you are working is very distracting.

10. To test your dog's training, try for ten in a row. If she gets less than 100 percent, go back to practicing before you ask for the behavior in that environment.

Remember to use the lure just to get the behavior started so that your dog does not become too dependent upon it.

If your dog fails the Ten in a Row rule, you need to help her for a few repetitions before she attempts the exercise again without help. Going back to the previous steps to help your dog get into the right position gives her information about what she needs to do to earn her click and treat and prevents her from getting confused and frustrated.

Teaching Sit/Stay

Turning the Sit into a Sit/Stay involves two processes: getting the dog to hold the position for longer periods of time (duration), and holding the position while the handler moves further away (distance). If you teach this behavior in two steps you will have a reliable behavior that is resistant to falling apart around distractions. The steps for teaching duration include the following.

1. Get your dog into a Sit and then count to two before you click and treat.
2. Gradually increase the time the dog has to hold the behavior by several seconds before you click and treat until you can build it up to ten seconds between each click and treat.
3. When you can get to ten seconds, go ahead and verbally label it Stay and give the hand signal. (Most people use a flat, open palm toward the dog.)
4. Increase the time between each click and treat randomly to keep the dog guessing as to how long she must wait for her next click.
5. Add in distractions, and start from the first step to rebuild the behavior of Sit/Stay around this new variable.

Try not to let your dog be wrong more than twice before helping her into the right position, lessening the distraction, or changing the variables. If your dog makes more than two mistakes in a row, you need to change something so that she can be right more easily.

The second part of the Sit/Stay command is for the dog to hold the sit while you move away from her. The steps for teaching your dog to hold her position relative to yours are:

1. Get your dog into a sit and take a small step right or left, returning immediately. If your dog maintains her position, click and treat. If she doesn't, do a smaller movement.
2. Gradually shift your weight, leaving your hands in front of the dog. Click and treat the dog for maintaining her position in front of you. Practice this gradual movement until the dog is convinced she should stay in one spot.
3. Increase the distance slowly and keep moving at first, never staying in one spot too long without coming back to the dog to click and treat. Standing still too soon in the process will cause your dog to run to you.
4. When your dog is able to maintain her position as you cross the room, start to stay away a few seconds longer before coming back.
5. Increase the time slowly so that you are combining both the length of time the dog holds the position (duration) and your distance from the dog.

Teaching Down/Stay

When you are teaching your dog to Lie Down and Stay for extended periods of time, pay attention to the surface that you are asking him to lie on. Make sure it isn't extreme in temperature and that it isn't so hard and uncomfortable that your dog fidgets and gets up a lot because it is too uncomfortable to stay down. Short-coated dogs are often very uncomfortable on hardwood or linoleum floors. They will learn to lie down more readily on a carpet or towel.

1. Starting with your dog in the Sit position, use a treat to lure her nose about halfway to the floor. When your dog follows the treat by lowering her head, click and treat.
2. Gradually lower your hand closer to the floor. You may need to go back to a food lure for a few reps if your dog seems stuck and won't lower her head any further.

3. When you get the treat to the floor, experiment with holding it out under your hand, or closer to and under her chest, and wait. Most dogs will fool around for a while trying to get the treat and then plop to the ground. When your dog goes all the way down, click and treat.

4. Repeat this six times with a treat, clicking and treating each time your dog goes all the way down.

5. Now, without a treat in your hand, make the same hand motion and click and treat your dog for any attempt to lie down.

6. If your dog fails more than twice, go back to using a treat for six more times and then try again.

7. Take it on the road. When you go somewhere new or involve distractions like other dogs and people, the behavior may fall apart a bit. Don't be afraid to go back to using a food lure to show the dog what to do and then fade it out when the dog is performing the behavior reliably.

Some dogs have trouble lying down and seem to get stuck in the sitting position. Here are some tips for dogs that get stuck.

- Practice on a soft surface away from distractions at first.
- Use novel treats that the dog loves but hardly ever gets.
- Use a low table, the rung of a chair, or even your outstretched leg to lure the dog low to the ground and under the object to give her the idea.
- Experiment with holding the treat closer to the dog's body and between the front paws close to the chest, or further away from her nose at a 45-degree angle.
- Avoid pushing on the dog to get her down. As soon as you start pushing and prodding, the dog turns her brain off and stops thinking about what she's doing, letting you do the work. If you want to teach your dog to think, don't push or pull her into position.

The most important thing to remember while training your dog, especially if you're struggling with a lesson, is to be patient and practice often.

Short, frequent sessions will be much more effective for you and your dog than marathon sessions.

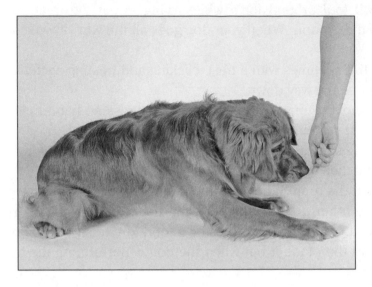

Wait until the dog's elbows hit the ground before clicking and giving up the treat.

Teaching Your Dog to Come

Teaching your dog to come when you call him has more to do with the status of your relationship than anything else you've done to this point. If your dog believes that you are in charge, she knows that you control everything good and that she must check in with you often to have access to the things she wants. Review the section on leadership earlier in this chapter and try to be diligent about becoming a strong and fair leader.

From a training perspective, the first thing a dog must do to Come is to turn away from what she wants and look back in your direction. To teach a strong foundation for Come, follow these steps:

1. Start with the dog on her leash in a slightly distracting area, keeping her from the things she wants, and wait for her to look back at you, then click and treat.
2. Repeat this until the dog no longer looks away from you.
3. Change the distraction, go somewhere more stimulating, or go closer to the distractions and repeat.

4. If your dog doesn't look back at you in thirty seconds or less, move further away from the distraction until she will look at you within that time.
5. When your dog is looking back at you predictably, run backward as you click and deliver the treat at your feet to encourage the dog to catch you.
6. As your dog gets good at this, wait until she is on her way back to you before you click.
7. Verbally label this behavior Come as your dog gets to you to eat her treat.
8. Change the distractions. Increase the intensity of a distraction by going closer to it or increasing the distance between you and your dog by using a longer leash.
9. If your dog doesn't respond by looking back in a reasonable amount of time, don't be afraid to back away from the distraction.

The trick to teaching Come is to set your dog up to be successful. Don't allow off-leash freedom if your dog is not reliable, and practice, practice, practice! After establishing a firm foundation for Come on a six-foot leash, use a longer leash and review all of the steps from the beginning. Some dogs will make great progress quickly, and others will need you to go much slower so that they can be successful.

ALERT!

Dogs are impulsive and love to chase things that run. Always be cautious about giving your dog freedom in unfenced areas. Your dog may be the best-trained dog in the neighborhood, but if a cat runs across the street she is likely to follow. Use a leash on all walks on city streets and be cautious when allowing off-leash freedom.

Gradually increase the length of the leash until your dog can turn away from what she wants (the foundation for coming when called) and come back to you easily. Progress to dropping the leash and letting her drag it, and eventually take it off while reviewing all the steps to teach Come. When you first take off the leash, you may want to practice in a fenced or protected area in case you've hurried your dog's training and she runs off and won't come. This means that you need to back up a few steps and put the leash back on for a while.

Though the process seems a bit long and tedious, it is well worth the effort of having a dog that comes reliably when you call it. As your dog gets good at checking in with you, you can begin to offer real life rewards mixed in with treats, like the freedom to go back to playing with another dog, the opportunity to sniff a smelly spot on the ground, or the chance to chase a squirrel. If these opportunities are given as rewards, your dog will learn that coming to you and checking in on a regular basis is a very good thing. Regardless of how well your dog learns to come when called however, remember never to allow her off leash in unsafe areas where a mistake could cost her her life.

Minimizing the Cue

In early training, the original cue you use to get the dog to perform is overexaggerated. When the trick is polished, change the cue to something more subtle or change a verbal cue to a hand signal instead.

To change the original signal to a new one, the order in which you introduce the new command is very important. The standard practice for introducing a new label is: new cue followed by old cue. If you don't put the new cue first, the dog will ignore it and continue to respond to the old cue. You won't be able to get rid of the old signal unless the new signal precedes it.

Roll Over is a good example of a trick where you might want to abbreviate the original cue or replace it all together. When you first start the training, you'd probably use a full arm circle type of motion close to the dog's body to get her to throw herself over. You'd eventually want to shorten that to a slighter circular motion or even a closed fist.

Steps to Success

Successful training depends on you—the leader—having a clear goal and a plan to get there.

Make a Plan and Chart Your Progress

Making a plan means breaking down each trick into individual steps and tracking or charting your dog's progress—and stumbling blocks. Get in the habit of examining your dog's success rate and periodically re-evaluate your shaping plan, making adjustments as necessary. Use the Ten in a Row rule as a general guide. If your dog can repeat a step with 100 percent accuracy, you are ready to progress to the next step. If your dog makes a lot of mistakes or acts disinterested, break things down into smaller steps or change your approach in some way.

Whenever you are teaching a new behavior, click and treat your dog frequently. If you find that you are waiting around awhile for your dog to offer the right behavior, you need to break the behavior down into smaller steps. As you teach each new commands, be sure that your dog has lots of opportunities to be right.

With each trick or behavior you teach, write each step down in sequential order and set small goals for each training session. Keeping your session short (less than ten minutes) with a clear goal in mind will help you determine whether you need to make things easier for your dog. A training log is an important part of a successful program, because your notes provide a bit of history on your progress. If you run into a snag along the way, you can review the steps where you were most successful, see what worked, and make changes so you can keep moving forward.

The Importance of Practice

Dogs learn things by repeating them over and over. The more you practice together, the better the dog will become at performing the behavior reliably and on cue. Dogs don't generalize well. Just because they can Lie Down on the first try in the kitchen doesn't mean they'll be able to Lie Down at the park or veterinarian's office.

The best way to ensure your dog's quick, reliable response to commands is to practice frequently in lots of different environments. The key to getting your dog to perform around distractions, like people and other dogs, is to introduce them slowly. Give the dog as much help as he needs to be successful. Dogs don't need to be corrected for not performing a behavior in a new environment; they need to be shown what to do until they can perform the behavior on their own. If you find the need to correct your dog, you haven't done a good enough job of setting him up for success. Go back to the drawing board and plan out your sessions again.

Working on the Quality of the Trick

Working on the quality of the trick is an important part of taking your tricks to the next level. The qualities of distance, speed, and duration will help you polish your tricks and let you expand them to more elaborate performances. Distance pertains to how far away from your dog you can be and still have him perform the trick, speed refers to how fast he can execute it, and duration indicates how long he'll hold it.

The key is to work on improving one aspect of your dog's performance at a time. For instance, if you want to teach your dog to wave to you at a distance, you would not ask him to hold the wave (duration) for any longer than he normally offers it. Similarly, you would not work him at a distance if you were trying to work on the duration of the wave. Separating these variables of trick training will help your dog learn faster, more consistently, and more reliably.

FACT

The simple truth of training dogs is that you get what you pay attention to. Set your dog up to succeed, limit his options, and reinforce what's going right, and you'll soon have a well-behaved dog that everyone loves to have around.

Distance

To increase the amount of space between you and your dog, you simply need to lower your standards for all other aspects of the trick except his ability to perform the behavior (however sloppy) at gradually increasing distances. Start with the dog close to you and reinforce him for gradually increasing distances. You will know if you have gone too far because he will make mistakes. This means you should shorten the distance until he is able to perform reliably and continue more slowly.

Once you have your dog working reliably at one distance, go ahead and gradually increase it until you are satisfied with the performance. Don't be afraid to go back to the beginning if your dog falls apart and you lose the behavior entirely. If you go back to the beginning and start again, your dog will catch on more rapidly and give you an even better performance.

Speed of Execution

The speed with which your dog performs a trick refers to the time between the moment you give the command and the time the dog actually starts to perform the behavior. To improve your dog's speed, it is helpful to pick a number of seconds in which he has to perform the trick and only reward those repetitions that fall within your time limit. Anything more gets ignored. It takes most dogs only a short time to realize that it is how fast they perform the behavior that counts. Don't forget that if you are working on speed, you should lower your standards for other aspects of the trick.

QUESTION?

What should you do if your dog refuses to perform a behavior you think he knows?
If your dog does not respond to a command you think he knows, show him again, using a food lure or hand motion to help. Repeat this half a dozen times and then try again. Dogs that don't respond to commands may be distracted in a new environment.

Duration

This aspect also refers to time, but it deals with the amount of time the dog must hold the behavior, such as leaving his paw up to wave, before you reward him. You can teach duration by delaying the click for varying amounts of time and only rewarding repetitions that are longer than average. As you increase the duration, go slowly so as not to lose the behavior altogether. If you increase the duration too fast and the dog no longer performs the behavior, go back to the beginning and start again. You will find that if you are flexible you will make an enormous amount of progress in a relatively short period of time.

Applying these tools as you go about teaching your dog any trick you choose will make it fun and interesting for your dog to learn them. Concentrate on teaching the basics using these common methods before you start teaching tricks. Having lots of options will make it more fun for you to train your dog and more fun for him to learn what you want to teach him. If you follow the simple plan outlined in this chapter for establishing yourself as the leader and teaching the basic commands of Sit/Stay, Down/Stay, and Come, you will reap the rewards of having a well-behaved member of your family.

CHAPTER 6

Kindergarten Tricks

Teaching tricks does not need to be a complicated task. Even novice trainers can teach a dog an entertaining trick, giving both trainer and dog a sense of accomplishment. The tricks that follow are simple and easy to teach. They are even appropriate for puppies, with their limited understanding of the training game.

Teaching Simple Tricks

Each dog has a unique style of learning, and it is your job as her trainer to find the best techniques to explain to her whatever trick you are trying to teach. The amount of sessions it will take to learn one trick will vary according to the dog, so just know that as long as you are progressing from one step to the next, you are succeeding. Some additional things to keep in mind as you work on new tricks with your dog include the following:

- Only introduce one new skill per session. Skipping around too much will confuse the dog and might discourage sensitive dogs altogether.
- Remember that the shaping outlines are building blocks toward an end goal. As with most goals, teaching a trick is accomplished by starting at the beginning with the first step and progressing through to the end by adding each step, one at a time, until all the steps come together to form a trick.
- Once you've established a few basics, it's a good idea to review previous skills or steps as a warm-up.
- Try to work in two or three sessions per day to see real improvement and accomplishment in a week's time, but there should be at least two hours between sessions.
- Dogs take time to process what they have learned, and sometimes a rest gives them time to put more challenging concepts together.

You can teach the following tricks most easily using one of the three tools mentioned in Chapter 4—luring, free shaping, or targeting. You may want to review the basics often to reinforce your general skills before attempting to teach these tricks.

Polite Pawing

Many dogs can do these simple tricks with very little prompting because they already use their paws to play with toys or get your attention. If your dog falls into that category, teaching these tricks should be fairly straightforward.

Give Your Paw

Give Your Paw may be the most natural trick for dogs prone to pawing. However, it also serves as the foundation for other paw-oriented tricks, so master this one first. The shaping steps for teaching Give Your Paw are:

1. Find out what usually gets your dog to paw at you and use it to get him to do it. As your dog's paw is in the air, click and treat.
2. Repeat this fifteen to twenty times until your dog is offering his paw readily.
3. Now, leave your hand outstretched and wait your dog out; don't prompt him in any other way and see what happens. If he lifts his paw at all, click and treat.
4. If after a few seconds he does not lift his paw, go back to helping him for another ten to fifteen repetitions before you try again. You want the dog to understand that lifting his paw is what gets the click and treat to happen.
5. If you are using your outstretched hand as the prompt that gets your dog to give his paw, this can be turned into the cue for the behavior. Show your hand and click and treat as your dog is stretching out his paw.

This trick may come in handy when teaching better greeting manners around guests.

6. Add the verbal cue Give Your Paw when your dog is raising his paw to slap your hand on a regular basis.
7. Practice in different environments with various distractions, being careful not to overwhelm your dog. If the behavior falls apart in the

new place, don't be afraid to make things easier for him and help him out.

8. Avoid repeating yourself over and over; give one cue, wait for your dog's response, and click and treat. If your dog's response is not quick enough, go back to helping him for six to eight repetitions before trying again.

If your dog does not usually raise his paw, try teasing him with a really yummy treat in your fist held at about nose height, scratching him on the chest, or touching his toenails with your finger. Most dogs will respond by raising a paw, giving you an opportunity to click and treat.

High Five

The High Five is just a variation of the Give Your Paw trick with a few minor adjustments.

1. Teach your dog to target your hand with her paw for a click and treat (see Chapter 4).
2. Present your hand as the target in various positions until you can hold your hand up, palm facing the dog with fingers toward the ceiling. Click and treat your dog for touching your hand with his paw.
3. Practice this until your dog is quickly raising his paw when he sees you put your hand up.
4. Verbally label the behavior High Five when it is happening on a regular basis.
5. Add in distractions and work on having your dog do it with other people as well.

Sometimes you'll want to use a different cue or hand signal than the one you started with when you are teaching tricks. There is an order that must be followed before your dog will perform the behavior on the new cue. You must present the new cue before the old cue or the dog will not pay attention to the new cue.

Wave

Teaching your dog to Wave is adorable and effective doggie PR because it gives him an appropriate way to greet people. Establishing an acceptable behavior, such as waving, is one of the keys to eliminating jumping. To perform this trick, the dog must raise a paw in the air while remaining stationary, which you can teach using a combination of targeting and shaping. The shaping steps are:

1. Start with your dog in a Sit/Stay and move a few steps away from him. Go back every few seconds for a full minute to reward your dog for not following you.
2. Standing in front of your dog, ask for his paw and click and treat him for giving it to you several times in a row.
3. Take a step away from your dog and ask for his paw. Click and treat the slightest effort to raise his paw without trying to move toward you. You may need to reward him for staying for a few repetitions before he'll remain in position and lift his paw.

To get a nice high Wave, remember to click when the dog is raising his paw rather than when his paw is coming back down.

4. As your dog raises his paw to place it in your outstretched hand, start fading this cue by removing your hand quickly. Click and treat your dog for swiping the air.

5. Repeat this step until your dog starts raising his paw when he sees your outstretched hand.

6. As your dog starts to offer swiping the air readily without moving forward, you can begin to verbally label this new behavior Wave.

7. Change the hand signal to an actual wave by changing the position of your hand from an outstretched palm to a waving hand. Offer the new cue (the waving hand) right before the old cue (the outstretched hand), gradually fading out the old cue until your dog is performing the behavior when you are waving at him.

8. Add in distractions and practice in new places until the behavior is reliable.

Calm Canines

Training involves many elements, but there are two things to remember. First, make the most of your dog's natural behavior, as the paw tricks demonstrate. Second, use training to elicit desired behavior, such as behaving in the presence of other people or dogs. The following tricks will help your dog remain calm and will put your guests at ease.

FACT

To make progress in trick training, you need to work at a pace where the dog is getting clicked and treated frequently. As you increase the difficulty of a trick, try not to let the dog make more than two or three mistakes before you show her what you want her to do.

Bow

Teaching your dog to Bow on command will make for a flashy trick and also may help you put a visiting dog at ease. Dogs invite each other to play in this position, and it can be an excellent way for your dog to learn to make friends. To perform this trick, the dog starts from a standing position and lowers the front half of her body until her elbows touch the floor. Here are the shaping steps:

1. Starting your dog in a standing position, hold your hand below her chin (about 3 inches) and get her to touch your hand, then click and treat.
2. Gradually make it harder by placing your hand closer to the ground in increments of several inches each time. Click and treat your dog for making an attempt to lower her head further to touch your hand.
3. When your hand is resting on the ground, click and treat your dog for touching it with her nose without lying all the way down. If your dog continually lies down, raise your hand by several inches for a while before continuing.
4. Make sure you watch your dog carefully and click and treat any effort she makes to bend her elbows.
5. Once your dog will lower her top half, start giving her less help by removing your target hand before she touches it.
6. Fade the hand target until she drops her head when you just begin to make the motion with your hand.
7. Increase the difficulty by only clicking and treating those repetitions where she lowers her head fast.
8. Increase the difficulty by increasing the duration (length of time the dog holds the behavior) by adding a Hold It or Stay command. To increase the duration of the behavior, delay the click by one or two seconds and gradually increase the time.

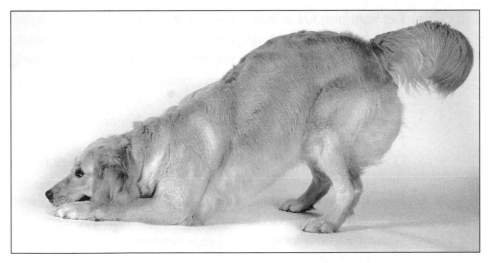

For a longer duration, try delivering the treat right between the front paws after the click.

9. Add a verbal cue like Bow just before she performs the behavior.
10. Take it on the road and perform in new places.

If you have a dog who insists on lowering her bottom half as well as her top, try luring the dog with a treat under a coffee table or chair. This often cures the dropped bottom.

FACT

Review Stay with your dog first; then gradually give the cue for the behavior at greater and greater distances, only moving further away if the dog performs the behavior reliably. Don't be afraid to do remedial work with Stay if the behavior seems to fall apart.

Play Dead

Teaching your dog to Play Dead is a show-stopping trick that is sure to make even non–dog lovers sit up and take notice. This trick requires the dog to lie on her back with her paws in the air and hold it until released.

1. Get your dog to Lie Down, then click and treat.
2. Use a treat to roll your dog onto her side, then click and treat.
3. Fade the lure by doing six repetitions in a row and then trying the seventh repetition without the lure, clicking and treating the dog for performing the behavior.
4. Reintroduce the lure to get her to roll onto her back, then click and treat. Fade the lure after the sixth repetition.
5. Go back and put all three steps together so that she performs them all in one continuous motion for one click and treat.
6. Fade the lure by working with food for six repetitions then without food for two repetitions. Go back and forth until your dog responds the same with or without food. Note: The way you hold your hand will become the exaggerated cue that starts the behavior.

7. Change the old cue to a new cue by offering the new cue before the motion you used to get the behavior started. Pointing your thumb and forefinger like a gun and saying "bang!" is very flashy!

8. Work on speed by only rewarding the dog for quick responses to the new signal. Decide on how many seconds she has to start the behavior and click and treat even before she finishes. Clicking in the middle of the behavior is what builds speed.

Belly Up

This is similar to the Play Dead trick except that it also involves allowing someone to touch the dog while she is flat on her back. Not all dogs are comfortable with this, so know your dog well before asking for it in front of strangers.

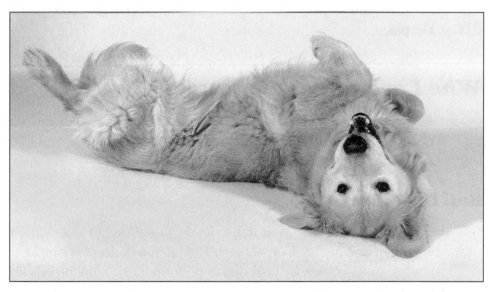

Teaching the Belly Up exercise can make grooming your dog a much easier process.

1. Have your dog Lie Down, then click and treat.
2. Lure your dog onto her side, then click and treat.
3. Lure your dog over onto one hip, then click and treat.
4. Lure your dog all the way onto her back, then click and jackpot (give a large number of small treats) the first time and quit the session.

5. Once your dog is rolling onto her back easily, fade the lure after six repetitions and see what happens. If the dog performs the Belly Up behavior, click and treat. If not, lure her six more times and try again.
6. When your dog is readily rolling onto her back, label it Belly Up just before she offers the behavior.
7. Delay the click once your dog is in the Belly Up position by at first a few seconds and then more and more until she will hold the position for longer periods of time.
8. Add in touching her belly and click and treat her for holding the Belly Up position while you do this.
9. Add in the distraction of strangers touching her belly, and click and treat her for holding the Belly Up position while being petted.
10. Take it on the road. Practice in new places with new people. Don't be afraid to help your dog into position if she gets confused in a new place.

Who Loves an Audience?

Although some of your training is behavior modification, some of it is just plain fun. Once you've trained a well-behaved, socially acceptable dog, let everyone in on the games!

Roll Over

Roll Over requires your dog to lie down flat on her stomach, roll all the way over, and get back on her feet. Though the concept is simple, this is not always an easy trick for your dog to perform. Long-back breeds like dachshunds or basset hounds may not be as good at this trick as other breeds due to the way they are built.

Pay close attention to your dog to be sure she's not hurting or twisting her back. If, despite your best efforts, your dog refuses to get on her back, skip this trick and try another. Your dog may be sore or uncomfortable and this may be her only way to express it. If possible, teach this trick on a soft surface like a towel or carpet so the dog is more comfortable.

1. Get your dog to lie down with her belly touching the ground and click and treat.
2. Use a treat or a toy to turn your dog's head until she flops over on one hip; click and treat.
3. Use a treat or toy held close to your dog's shoulder to get her completely on her side; click and treat.
4. Gradually move the treat or toy, while she's chewing on it, to move her onto her back and then eventually all the way over. (This step often takes many attempts before the dog is comfortable enough to be on her back.)
5. Click and treat small efforts to move toward the treat at first before you get her to move further to get her click and treat. If you make it too hard to earn a click, your dog will quit on you and think it's no fun.
6. When your dog is rolling over easily, it's time to start fading out all the extra cues and make her offer more before you click.

Be sure to click while the dog is in motion to improve the speed of the rollover.

7. Once she can roll over with just this little bit of help, you can begin to verbally label this trick Roll Over. Whatever you are doing with your hand or fist could be a hand signal for the behavior as well.

8. Add in distractions one at a time and be prepared to help your dog complete the trick if she has trouble concentrating.

ALERT!

Dogs with long backs sometimes find it uncomfortable and awkward to roll over onto their backs and then try to get back on their feet. Overweight dogs or dogs that have had back injuries in the past may also have difficulties.

Spin

Spinning involves your dog turning in a complete circle in either direction. As your dog gets good at this, you can have her keep spinning until you tell her to stop. If you've tried to teach this trick using a lure or food treat, you probably realized how difficult it is to get rid of the lure. Instead, use targeting either with your hand or with a target stick to show your dog what you want her to do.

1. With your dog facing you, use your hand as a target to get her to follow your hand a quarter of the way around, then click and treat.

2. Now, leave your target hand at the quarter-way mark and wait until your dog touches it with her nose on her own before you click and treat. Practice this until she's offering it readily.

3. Next, just before she touches your hand, move your target hand to the halfway point and click and treat your dog for following it, but before she actually touches it.

4. At this point, as you drop your hand she may spin the rest of the way around, but continue to click and treat for the halfway point in order to build speed.

5. Use your target hand to start the dog turning, but then pull it away quickly. Click and treat your dog for attempting to turn without the target to guide her.

6. Time the click so that you're clicking the dog for being at the halfway point.
7. Continue to minimize your target hand and click the dog for continuing to turn without your help.
8. Fade the target hand to just a motion to the left or right.
9. Fade the target to a simple left or right cue. A pointed index finger would be appropriate as a final signal.

Once you and your dog have mastered ten in a row, you can begin working on speed. (See Chapter 5.) Set a time limit in which your dog must perform the behavior, and click and treat only those repetitions that meet the goal. To train your dog to spin in the other direction, simply go back to the first step and work your way through.

Are You Scared?

This trick will put a smile on everyone's faces, especially children's. To indicate his "fright," the dog runs under a table or bed and peeks out from under the tablecloth or bedspread. The shaping steps for teaching Are You Scared? are:

1. Start with your dog under the table, and use your voice or a treat to get him to peek out. Click and treat.
2. Make sure you time your click for when he first pushes out from under the cloth.
3. Repeat this six to eight times and then try putting him under again and waiting to see if he offers peeking out on his own.
4. Once your dog has this part down, teach him to go under the table using a target lid. (See Chapter 4 for teaching targeting with a lid.)
5. Bait the target with a treat at first to encourage him to go under the tablecloth and click and treat each time.
6. Take the bait off the target but leave the target under the table or bed and send him again. Click and treat your dog for going under the table or bed after the target.
7. To get the peeking behavior, repeat the previous step until your dog offers it readily and then delay the click. When your dog doesn't hear

the click, he will probably come back out to see what's wrong. Click and treat him just as he peaks out from under the cloth.

8. Repeat this until he runs under and peeks out readily; then verbally label the behavior Are You Scared?

QUESTION?

What if my dog doesn't peek?
If you're having trouble getting your dog to peek because he runs all the way out from under the tablecloth or bedspread, it means you need to click sooner. An early click will catch the dog just as he is emerging and give him the idea that peeking is what is being clicked.

Who's a Brave Dog?

This trick is similar to Are You Scared? except in this trick the dog runs around behind the handler and through his legs until he is looking up at the handler's face. The shaping steps to teach Who's a Brave Dog? are:

1. Starting with your dog sitting in front of you, use a target stick (see Chapter 4) to get your dog to go around you to the left or right.
2. Practice this until your dog will run behind your legs and touch the target for a click and treat.
3. Slowly move the target between your feet so that your dog comes between your legs enough to be able to look up at you.
4. Withhold the click after your dog starts to catch on to going through your legs and see if he will look up at you, then click and treat.
5. If your dog runs all the way through your legs, use the target stick to show him where to stop and click and treat him before he actually touches it.
6. You can label this behavior Who's a Brave Dog? by saying the label right before you give the cue that starts the behavior, like pointing or whatever you did to encourage the dog to go around you.

7. Slowly fade the target as your dog starts to offer the behavior readily by showing the target to get him started and then making the target disappear.

8. Add distractions and be sure to go back to helping your dog with the target stick if the behavior falls apart.

Looking worried is a practiced skill for this beautiful girl.

Regardless of your dog's skill level, anyone can have fun teaching these simple tricks. Remember, the bottom line is to make sure you have fun while spending time with your best friend. Whether you teach your dog tricks to entertain your friends and family or you do therapy work in hospitals and nursing homes, having a dog that can do tricks shows off all his amazing attributes. Spending time together learning something new will enhance your bond and strengthen your relationship, making the quality of life better for both of you.

Social Graces

So your dog will shake hands and bow—that's something! Well, you can certainly expand her social skills to include a few kisses and pleasant conversation. The joy of having a dog is your interaction with each other. These next two behaviors really make the most of that.

Kiss Me

Teaching this behavior utilizes a combination of free shaping and luring. You are catching the dog in the act of doing the behavior and rewarding it, but you are getting the behavior started by prompting it first. The shaping steps for teaching Kiss Me are:

1. Using food to initially excite your dog is the key. Feed her a few small pieces of a treat and eat a few yourself, then stick your chin out and wait.
2. At the first sign of any attempt to open her mouth to lick you, click and treat.
3. Try putting the treats in your mouth and showing her they're there. Click and treat any attempt to lick you.
4. Add the verbal cue Kiss right before you think she's going to offer the behavior. Click and treat as the behavior happens.

There's nothing like a kiss from a good friend to cheer you up!

5. Fade the food by showing it to the dog and putting it away on a counter or table and commanding Kiss. When she kisses, click and treat and run to get the treat.
6. Repeat this until the dog is beginning to offer the kiss as soon as you stick out your chin.

Speak

Luring and free shaping, or a combination of the two, are the best tools for teaching this trick. The trick itself requires your dog to bark on cue.

1. Find something that causes your dog to bark, like a knock on the door or holding a treat out of range. Click and treat her when she barks.
2. Repeat at least twenty to twenty-five times.
3. Fake the antecedent to barking (the knock), and if your dog starts to bark, click and treat.
4. Verbally label the behavior Speak just before your dog barks.
5. Don't click and treat for any barking other than the one you ask for.
6. If your dog barks at inappropriate times, be obvious about turning your upper body away to let her know that extraneous barking will not be rewarded.

Experimenting with different types of rewards will make you a more versatile and successful dog trainer. Experiment with food rewards, games, toys, and social opportunities, such as letting your dog say hello to a person after your dog performs Sit. Know where and when to use these to improve your dog's training program.

After basic obedience training skills (Sit, Stay, and Come), these simple tricks are the best opportunity for you and your dog to build a trusting and cooperative relationship. You'll develop a better understanding of how your dog thinks and what motivates her, and your dog will learn to read your cues. Take the time to train your dog well. You'll both get the best results that way.

CHAPTER 7

Retrieving Tricks

Any dog can learn to pick something up in his mouth and bring it to her handler. Although some dogs have an instinctive talent to perform this behavior, even the most reluctant dog can learn to retrieve using operant conditioning by means of a clicker and treats.

Shaping the Retrieve

To shape the process of retrieving, break it down into tiny increments. Even dogs that are retrieving fanatics may refuse to pick up certain objects like keys or tools. Teaching a shaped retrieve using operant conditioning will make your dog a reliable retriever, and it will also give you a strong base for teaching the retrieving tricks that follow.

QUESTION?

What is the difference between operant and classical conditioning?
Operant conditioning (click and treat) recognizes, and therefore encourages, desired behavior. Classical conditioning creates positive associations between two events.

When shaping a dog to retrieve, it is best to pick an easy object to start with, something the dog is likely to pick up on his own. If you're not sure what texture appeals to your dog, set out a bunch of objects and see which he chooses to play with on his own. Most dogs don't like to pick up metal and have difficulty picking up small objects that require them to smoosh their noses into the floor trying to get their mouths around it. Choose something your dog can get his mouth around easily, such as a face cloth, a retrieving dumbbell, or a small empty box.

Using a novel object will make it more likely that your dog will at least investigate it, giving you a starting point for shaping the retrieve. Teach the retrieve by breaking it down into the most basic steps so that it won't fall apart later. The shaping steps to teach the retrieve are as follows:

1. Put an item on the floor about three feet away from your dog.
2. Click and treat him for moving toward it.
3. Click and treat him for touching the object with his nose.
4. Repeat this step about a dozen times and then withhold the click.
5. If he mouths the object at all, click and treat.
6. Once your dog is mouthing the object, withhold the click until he picks up the object.
7. Delay the click once more and build the time he will hold the object.

8. Add distance by putting the object a short distance away at first and gradually increasing it.
9. Label the retrieve Take It as the dog is picking up the object.
10. Label the release of the object Give or Leave It.

When you are training for retrieving exercises, use an object that you can put away when the session is over. Keep the item "special" so that your dog looks forward to working with it every time you practice.

Links and Chains

As tricks get more complicated, you realize that one command really represents several behaviors—a behavior chain. In training your dog to perform these more complicated tasks, you can use two approaches: the behavior chain or back chaining. Really, the only difference is whether you start with first things first or work your way backward from a successful conclusion.

Behavior Chains

The concept of a behavior chain is relatively simple. In order for your dog to bring her leash to you on the command Go Get Your Leash, she must know where to find the leash, take it in her mouth (which may mean picking it up off the floor or pulling it from a doorknob), carry it to you in her mouth, and release it into your hand. Each of these steps is a link in the behavior chain, which is only as strong as its weakest element.

If your dog doesn't know how to carry objects without a lot of extra commands and prompting, behavior chain tricks will be choppy and uninteresting. Breaking things down into their component parts is a way of simplifying the trick and improving your dog's performance of it. A behavior chain is simply the breakdown of what the dog has to do to complete the behavior.

Back Chaining

Back chaining is related to behavior chains except instead of training step 1, step 2, step 3, you train it backward—step 3, step 2, step 1. The idea is that if you train something backward, your dog will perform the behavior more reliably and with greater speed and enthusiasm because she is moving toward something she already knows well. By teaching her a multistep task backward, you are helping her remember the steps more easily because she learned the last one first. So in the case of the trick Bring Me Your Leash, it would be hold the leash and release it into my hand, carry the leash to me from a distance, take it in your mouth, go find it.

Each of these steps may need to be broken down further to meet your dog's individual needs, but the basic concept is the same. When the dog performs the whole trick, she will be moving from less familiar steps to more familiar steps. Because she learned the last part of the trick first, she will be more confident and flashy as she gets to the end and more reliable overall in her performance of the trick.

Wait for your dog to get frustrated enough to actually close his mouth on the object before you click and treat. More than likely, he will mouth the object quickly and release it, so be ready to click and give a jackpot.

The Retrieving Tricks

Each of these tricks involves the dog retrieving or picking up something in her mouth and transferring it to another person. If your dog has any difficulty picking up the prop you are using, don't be afraid to go back to the basic steps of the retrieve using the new object. You will find that going back to kindergarten will help your dog's overall grasp of retrieving and will make him less likely refuse to cooperate.

Go Get Your Leash

This trick involves having your dog retrieve his leash and bring it to you. To make this easier on the dog you may want to have one place that you leave your dog's leash, like on a doorknob or by the front door. The dog has to go to where the leash is kept and pull the leash off with his mouth. He needs to carry the leash to you and hold it until you take it from him.

If you come across an object that your dog refuses to retrieve, go back and reshape the retrieve using this object. If the retrieving part of the trick is weak because the dog is not comfortable retrieving this particular object, the performance of the trick will become sloppy and unreliable.

If you teach this and the following behaviors using back chaining, you will find it easier for your dog to perform them because he is always moving toward the more familiar steps. Here are the shaping steps:

1. Hold the leash out and ask your dog to take it. Click and treat the exact moment he puts it in his mouth.
2. Back up a step and see if he will follow you; click and treat him for moving with the leash in his mouth.
3. Put the leash on the floor and tell him to Take It. As soon as he picks it up, click and treat.
4. Put the leash on the floor but don't click and treat until he takes it and takes several steps toward you.
5. Put the leash in various places at various distances and repeat. Click and treat for taking it under these new circumstances.
6. Gradually move the leash to where your dog can expect to find it and click and treat him for going to that spot.
7. Replace the Take It cue with Leash, by saying the new cue Leash right before the old cue. Gradually fade Take It so that your dog will perform the behavior on the new cue.

Get the Mail/Newspaper

This trick works well if you have a door slot for your mail or you have a daily newspaper that gets delivered to your door. For this trick, your dog has to go to where the mail or paper is kept, pick up the item, bring it to you, and release it into your hand. Here are the shaping steps:

He'll carry the paper and doesn't require a tip!

1. Teach your dog to carry nonessential letters and junk mail without stopping to shred them before you use the real thing. ("The dog ate the mortgage bill" probably won't go over well with your spouse.) Do this by clicking and treating your dog for taking the letter or newspaper and holding it without mouthing it.
2. Take a step or two away and have him bring it to you. Click and treat the motion of moving toward you.
3. Put the letter on the floor and tell your dog to Take It. You may want to use junk mail for this part until your dog refines his techniques in picking up something so close to the floor.

4. When your dog is retrieving with finesse, begin to work him with the real mail pile or newspaper.
5. Label this behavior Mail or Paper by saying this new cue right before the current cue Take It; pretty soon your dog will be fetching with enthusiasm and finesse.

Go Find the Remote

Visitors, especially those with only a mild interest in dogs, love this trick. Guests are always impressed when a dog can serve a useful purpose. If your housemate tends to hog the remote control, your dog can be your advocate in getting it back with a smile. For this trick, the dog has to find the remote, pick it up, carry it to you, and drop it in your hand.

1. Hand your dog the remote and click and treat him for holding it.
2. Back away a step or two and click and treat him for carrying it to you.
3. Put the remote on the couch or coffee table and tell your dog to Take It. Click and treat him for picking it up in his mouth.
4. Send him into the living room at greater distances and click and treat him when he finds the remote.
5. Call him to you as he gets the hang of this and click and treat him for holding it until you reach out to take it.
6. Replace Take It with the command Remote by offering the new cue right before the old cue "Take It."

Go Get the Phone

Nothing is better than having your own personal answering service. For this trick your dog has to go and retrieve the phone and bring it back to you. You may want to use a cordless phone for this and store it on a low table or the floor to make it easy for your dog to reach it.

Using a cordless phone for this trick is ideal, but you may want to start practicing with the receiver from an old phone to prevent damage to your existing one. Once the dog is pretty good at picking up the receiver without damaging it, make sure you make the real thing easily accessible to prevent dropping it or knocking it off a table.

1. Hand your dog the receiver and tell her to Take It. Click and treat your dog for taking it in his mouth and holding it for a few seconds.
2. Hand your dog the phone and back away from him, encouraging him to follow you. Click and treat him for carrying the phone to you. Make sure the click happens while he is moving toward you, not when he arrives.
3. Repeat this step again, but now click and treat your dog for delivering the phone to you.
4. Put the phone on the floor and ask him to Take It; click and treat him for picking up the phone.
5. Put the phone at greater distances and have him retrieve it from further away. Time the click and treat for when your dog puts his mouth on the phone.
6. Increase the difficulty by delaying the click until he has the phone and is turning back to you. You can use a voice prompt like his name or the Come command.
7. Label the behavior Get the Phone by saying it right before the commands Take It and Come, until you can gradually fade the old commands and replace them with the new command Go Get the Phone.
8. Practice in short sessions until your dog begins to move toward the phone on the command Go Get the Phone.

When teaching your dog to retrieve the phone, practice leaving it on a low table so your dog has easy access to it.

Go Get Your Dish

This trick is a great way to show off your dog's intelligence. You'll probably want to keep his food dish in one spot so that he knows where to go to get it. For this trick your dog goes and brings his empty dish to you. Some dogs find it hard to retrieve metal dishes, in which case you may want to use a plastic one instead. If you decide to use the metal dish, don't be afraid to review the retrieving steps with this new object. The shaping steps are as follows:

1. Hand your dog his dish and tell him to Take It. Click and treat him for holding the dish.
2. Take a step away and call him to you. Click and treat him for moving toward you with the dish in his mouth.
3. Put the dish on the floor and tell him to Take It; click and treat him for picking up the dish.
4. Repeat this step but back away and click and treat the dog for picking up the dish and moving toward you.
5. Put the dish closer and closer to where you normally keep it and send him to take it over greater distances.
6. As your dog gets good at this, replace Take It with the new verbal cue Wanna Eat? by saying the new cue right before the old cue, until the dog starts the behavior on the new cue.

FACT

Some dogs hate having anything metal in their mouths. For these dogs you may want to go back to kindergarten and reteach a retrieve with a metal object. See the shaping steps for teaching the retrieve and substitute the object with the metal bowl.

Find My Car Keys Please

If you constantly lose your keys, this trick may save you a lot of time. Your dog has to use his eyes and sense of smell to locate your keys. Then he will pick them up, bring them to you, and release them into your outstretched hand. The shaping steps are as follows:

1. Hand your dog your keys and tell him to Take It. Click and treat him for holding your keys.
2. Take a few steps back and call him to you. Click and treat him for moving toward you with the keys in his mouth.
3. Put the keys on the floor and tell him to Take It; click and treat him for picking up the keys.
4. Repeat the previous step but back away. Click and treat him for picking up the keys and moving toward you.
5. Put the keys in different places at varying distances and click and treat your dog for finding them. Vary where you put them, sometimes leaving them out in the open, sometimes leaving them concealed.
6. Gradually work it so that your dog is actively searching for your keys. When you are at this point, go ahead and label it Keys. Replace Take It by giving the new cue Keys right before the old cue. Then, gradually fade the old cue.
7. Practice this one frequently to keep your dog motivated about searching for your keys.

Take retrieving on the road right away. Performing retrieving tricks in public is difficult; if you practice in different places from the start, your dog will be comfortable retrieving anywhere.

Delivery Tricks

The fundamental skill involved in retrieval tricks is the dog's ability to carry things in her mouth. The secondary skill is the dog's ability to carry things in her mouth from one place to another. Delivery tricks simply exchange the "from" and "to," which, as these next few tricks will show, can be fun *and* functional.

Put Away Your Toys

This trick will impress your more practical non-dog-owning friends. A dog that picks up her own toys beats the heck out of a spouse or child who can't find the laundry hamper or put his dirty dishes in the sink. For this trick the dog has to pick up one toy at a time and put it in her toy box or basket. The shaping steps are as follows:

If only we could teach the human kids to do the same!

1. Hand your dog a toy and tell her to Take It; when she has the toy in her mouth, click and treat her for holding it.
2. Put the toy box between your feet and encourage the dog to come to you; click and treat her for holding the toy over the top of the box.
3. Repeat the previous step but ask the dog to Leave It as she holds the toy over the box.
4. Put the toy on the floor and tell her to Take It; click and treat her for picking up the toy.
5. Repeat the previous step with more than one toy on the floor at a time.
6. Replace the Take It and Leave It cues with the new cue Toys Away by saying the new cue right before the old cue. Gradually fade the old cue.

Bring This to Daddy

This trick is great for dogs looking for a job to do. Having your very own canine delivery service is a great way for your dog to earn her keep. For this trick your dog has to pick up an object—a note, a tool, or any item reasonable for her to carry—and take it to someone else in the house. The shaping steps are as follows:

1. Hand your dog an object, using the command Take It, and have a helper call her from a step or two away. Click and treat her for moving toward that person.
2. Gradually move the helper greater and greater distances and click and treat the dog for moving away from you and toward your helper.
3. Gradually fade out the helper calling the dog and have the person go out of sight.
4. Replace the Take It command with Bring This to Daddy by saying the new cue right before you say Take It. Click and treat the dog for taking the object and moving in the direction of the helper. Gradually fade out the old cue.
5. Vary the objects you have the dog carry and practice often. This is the type of trick that gets better the more you practice it.

Being a good dog trainer involves good planning. Trainers who plan ahead and map out their training sessions tend to have more success than those who don't. Clear goals and clear steps for reaching them are essential to knowing when your dog has arrived!

Mail a Letter

Teaching your dog to mail a letter is a fun and functional trick that uses lots of energy and is entertaining to watch. Your dog must take a letter in her mouth, jump on the mailbox, and push the letter through the slot. She will need you to pull down the lever for her so she can drop the mail in the right spot. This trick is probably best taught to dogs tall enough to reach the top of the mailbox, unless you give your little one a boost. The shaping steps for teaching this trick are as follows:

1. Using the Touch command, ask your dog to use her nose to push the letter into the slot. Click and treat her for touching her nose to the letter.
2. Withhold the click and treat until she pushes the letter a little further toward the slot this time.
3. Have her put two front paws on the mailbox and click and treat her for staying up for gradually longer periods of time. If you have a small dog, you may want to hold her close to the box and click her for putting her feet on the top.
4. Hand your dog a letter and tell her to Take It. Click and treat her for taking the letter, then for holding the letter for longer periods of time.
5. Call her to put her paws on the box while holding the letter and click and treat.
6. Work on this step until the dog is easily balancing on her hind legs while holding the letter.
7. Now try to get the dog to leave the letter on the tray by telling her to Leave It and clicking and treating her for letting the letter go. You may need to adapt this trick for small dogs by holding them close to the box.
8. Practice all the steps until the whole thing is fluid and the dog responds to your command Take It by following through with all the other steps.
9. Replace the cue Take It with the new cue Mail It by saying the new cue right before the old cue and gradually fading the old cue.

Throw This in the Trash

Teach your dog to pick up anything you point to, including soda cans or other household items. This retrieving trick requires your dog to pick up the trash and release the object into a trash bucket. To make it easier for your dog to get the trash into the container, you will probably want to use an open or swing-top trash bucket that is no taller than your dog's elbows.

1. Have your dog retrieve lots of different kinds of trash items, and have her bring them to you over increasingly longer distances.
2. Sit on a chair with the trash bucket between your feet. Tell your dog to pick up an item using the Take It cue and call her to you; click and treat her when she is as close to the opening of the bucket as she'll come.
3. Repeat this step but delay the click by a few seconds until she is eventually standing with her chin right over the edge of the bucket.
4. With your dog standing close to the bucket, tell her to Leave It and click and treat her for releasing the trash. You will need to practice this so that your dog will eventually release the item right into the trash bucket.
5. Experiment by withholding the click until your dog makes a deliberate effort to drop the item into the bucket.
6. Label the behavior Throw It Away by saying this new cue right before the old cues Take It and Leave It. You will have to practice this many times before the new cue initiates the behavior.
7. Practice with different items so that your dog will retrieve and discard just about anything you ask her to.

Starting with a shallow box or basket will help the dog deliver the trash into the right spot.

The Next Level

Just when you think you've covered pretty much everything, new games and tricks come along to keep you and your pet learning together. Play them in your backyard, at the beach, or in the living room. Your dog is part of your family; if he's well trained and well behaved, he'll be treated as such.

FACT

Consider the height of the trash bucket and its opening when you are teaching this trick. The height of the bucket needs to be proportionate to the dog's head so the opening is easily accessible. As you add distance to this trick, you may even want to weight the basket so that it doesn't tip and scare the dog.

Let's Play Ring Toss

This old-fashioned game is a wonderful way to occupy a high-energy dog. For this trick the dog has to pick up each ring and place it on the post one at a time. This behavior is repeated until all three rings are on the post. You can buy an inexpensive ring toss game in any toy or department store. The shaping steps for this trick are as follows:

1. Hand your dog a ring and click and treat him for holding it.
2. Put the post close to you and have the dog deliver the ring close to the post. Click and treat him for releasing it over the post.
3. You may help the dog by tapping the post and encouraging him to drop it. Click and treat him for gradually closer attempts to leave the ring close to the post.
4. Withhold the click and treat and only click attempts to put the ring on the post. Once the dog is able to find the post on his own, add a label just before he drops the ring over the post. You can choose any label you like.

With patience and time, this can be a very entertaining game for your dog to play.

Sea Hunt

For this trick, your dog has to fetch things out of a body of water. You can use a baby pool, the bathtub, a bucket, or a lake or pond. The goal for the dog is to retrieve all the items you sink or float and bring them back to dry land. This is a terrific warm-weather game because it gives your dog a great way to cool off. Fill up a baby pool with a few inches of water and sink some treasures for him to retrieve. The shaping steps for teaching your dog to play Sea Hunt are as follows:

1. Hold an object on the surface and ask the dog to Take It. Click and treat him for putting his mouth around it.
2. Hold the item just below the surface and click and treat the dog for dipping his nose under and taking it.
3. Gradually hold the item deeper until the dog is snagging it off the bottom.
4. Vary what you have the dog retrieve and keep the game light and fun.
5. Vary the depth of the water as your dog gets better at this game to make it more interesting and fun for everyone involved. Once the dog is grabbing the object easily without much help from you, add the cue/label Take It just before the dog puts his mouth on the object.

Achoo! Can I Have a Tissue?

This trick is a real crowd pleaser. To perform this trick, the dog has to retrieve a tissue on a sneeze cue. Who wouldn't be amazed by a dog getting you a tissue when you sneeze? For this trick you need a pop-up box of tissues and a convincing fake sneeze. The shaping steps for teaching this trick are as follows:

1. Hand the dog a tissue and click and treat him for taking it and holding it.
2. Take a step away and have him bring it to you. Click and treat him for moving toward you with the tissue in his mouth.

3. Introduce the tissue box by pulling a tissue out and placing it across the top of the box. Click and treat the dog for taking the tissue off the top of the box.

4. Gradually tuck the tissue in so the dog has to pull the tissue out to get his click and treat.

5. Replace the old cue Take It with the new cue Achoo! by saying the new cue right before the old cue.

6. Click and treat the dog for starting the behavior as you sneeze.

Achoooooo!

Teach your dog to grab a tissue without tearing it into a million pieces by giving him lots of opportunities to practice and by not letting him hold the tissue for too long. You may also want to keep the tissue box in one place so the dog knows where to go to get a tissue when you sneeze.

Retrieving tricks are some of the most impressive because they involve several steps and highlight a dog's ability to think things through to put together a great performance. Each trick involves different props, but they all involve the same basic skill of being able to pick something up and carry it back to you. Reviewing the basic retrieve with the new item is a great way to warm up any new trick regardless of how experienced your dog is.

CHAPTER 8

Show-Off Tricks

We all have a little show-off in us, and dogs are no exception. Dogs love to make us laugh, and their antics often cheer us and relieve the stresses of everyday life. Taking the time to work with your dog will strengthen your bond with him and fine-tune your ability to communicate with each other. Your dog will love strutting his stuff.

Fancy Dogs

Some dogs, because of their breeds or their personalities, just seem to be suited to elegant tricks. That's why it's so important to know your dog and understand her—so you can train her to her best advantage.

Strike a Pose

When your dog is performing this trick, she looks as though she is posing for a picture. This trick requires your dog to turn her head to the side and hold it. The easiest way to teach this trick is by free shaping, which means limiting the dog's options and catching the right behaviors with a click and treat to shape the dog into the actual position you are looking for.

1. Start with your dog facing you in a Sit and click and treat her for staying.
2. After about thirty seconds, stop clicking and watch her closely; if she turns her head at all, click and treat.
3. Pick one side to start with and click any head turns in that direction.
4. When your dog starts to understand that turning her head is causing the click, delay the click by a few seconds to encourage her to hold position.
5. Gradually increase the length of time until your dog will turn her head to the side and hold it for fifteen seconds.
6. Label the behavior Pose just before she offers the turn of her head. Repeat until the command Pose causes the behavior.

Push a Baby Carriage

This trick is adorable, but for safety's sake it should not be practiced with a real baby. A doll carriage with a baby doll is safer for the dog as well. This trick requires the dog to stand and walk on her hind legs while pushing the carriage with her front feet. The shaping steps for teaching Push a Baby Carriage are as follows.

1. Start out by getting your dog to sniff the baby carriage, click and treat.
2. Secure the carriage so that it won't roll, and use a target to get your dog to put her front paws on the handle; click and treat.

3. Get your dog to hold the position by delaying the click and treat by a second or two.
4. Fix the carriage so that it will roll only a short distance (use blocks of wood behind the wheels), and click and treat your dog for moving the carriage a little at a time. Encourage your dog to move the carriage and click and treat her for complying.
5. Control how far the carriage rolls to avoid scaring your dog.
6. You can label this behavior Push by saying this cue as the dog is moving the carriage.

To prevent the carriage from tipping, weight the seat with some heavy books so that the carriage stays stable and stationary when your dog jumps up to touch the handle. Be sure the wheels are locked or use wooden blocks to prevent the carriage from rolling away too soon.

Hi-Ho, Silver, Away!

This trick, inspired by a horse-loving friend, is a great way to show off a dog that likes to jump up on you. The only difference is your dog is not making physical contact with you when she is holding the rearing-horse position with her front legs stretched upward. The shaping steps for teaching Hi-Ho, Silver, Away! are as follows:

1. Hold your hand as a target above your dog's head and click and treat her for touching it.
2. Gradually raise your hand until she is all the way up on her hind legs.
3. Practice frequently to help her build up her leg muscles.
4. Get your dog to hold the position by delaying the click and treat several seconds.
5. Increase the time by a few seconds until she can hold the position for about fifteen seconds.
6. Cue your dog to extend her paws by using the Give Your Paw command.

Break this trick down into short practice sessions to give the dog time to build up the muscles she needs to hold herself up.

7. Only click and treat versions of this behavior that are of longer duration and the right position (front paws extended).
8. Fade the hand target by using it to start the behavior and then pulling it away. Click and treat your dog for continuing to perform the behavior in the absence of the target.
9. Replace the old cue with the new cue Away by saying the new cue right before the dog starts the behavior.

Sit Up Pretty

For this trick, the dog is sitting on her hind legs with her front paws tucked into her chest. This is also a behavior that the dog needs to practice frequently to be able to build up her back and hind-end muscles.

Frequent short practice will allow your dog time to build up her rear end muscles and learn to balance herself.

The shaping steps for teaching Sit Up Pretty are as follows:

1. Use your hand as a target and click and treat her for touching your hand while raising her front end off the ground.
2. Withhold the click and treat by a few seconds to get your dog to hold the position high enough to have her sitting up on her back end but not standing.

3. Add a cue like Sit Up or Beg by saying it right before the Touch cue.
4. The click and treat should happen as soon as the dog starts the behavior on the new cue.

Practice fading your hand as a target by presenting it but clicking before your dog actually touches it. By clicking your dog early so that she is on her way to touching your hand but doesn't actually make contact with it, she will be less dependent on its presence, and it will be easier to fade.

Balance a Cookie on Your Nose

This trick demonstrates your dog's willpower, because she must balance a cookie on her nose and wait to take the cookie until you say so.

1. Start with your dog in a Sit in front of you and click and treat her for staying.
2. Practice holding her muzzle and placing a cookie on her nose for a click and treat.
3. Repeat this last step until the dog can hold still for several seconds.
4. Slowly let go of your dog's muzzle and click and treat her for holding it steady.
5. Gradually increase the amount of time your dog balances the cookie on her nose before you click and treat.
6. After a bit of practice, you will probably find that your dog develops a flip-and-catch technique to eat the cookie. This makes the trick all the more flashy and impressive.

Humble Dogs

Although some dogs are prone to fancier tricks, others are, by nature, more sedate. These simple and adorable tricks suit their personalities, and will therefore be easier for you to teach.

Say You're Sorry

For this trick the dog lies down with his chin on the ground between his front paws. An added bonus is teaching him to look up at you, which will add an even more convincing element to the performance. You may want to use this as the canine version of time out.

1. Put your dog in a Down, facing you; click and treat him for holding that position.
2. After about thirty seconds, withhold the click and wait. Pay close attention and click and treat any head motion down.
3. Once your dog starts to understand that lowering his head is what causes the click, withhold the click until your dog holds the position for an extra second.
4. Increase the number of seconds your dog has to keep his head down until you can build it up to fifteen to twenty seconds.
5. Label the behavior Sorry by saying the command right before he offers the behavior.
6. Repeat this step until the command Sorry triggers the behavior.

To help your dog understand that lowering his head causes the click, deliver the treat low to encourage the dog to look down. This will give you more opportunities to reward him for offering the right behavior.

Say Your Prayers

Any dog looks cute performing this trick. This trick requires your dog to rest his paws on a chair or stool and tuck his head between his front paws. He can be sitting or standing.

1. Use a table, stool, or chair that won't move when your dog puts his paws on it.
2. Get your dog to put his front paws on the stool by tapping the stool or luring him with a treat. Click any effort to get his paws up on the stool.
3. Delay the click so that your dog is putting his paws up and leaving them there for three seconds before you click and treat.

4. Using a yogurt lid as a target, get your dog to put his head between his front paws by placing the target slightly under his chest. Click and treat your dog for making attempts to touch the target.

5. Delay the click again until your dog holds his nose to the target for longer periods of time.

6. Fade the target slowly by clicking before he actually touches it, or by making it smaller.

7. Label the behavior Say Your Prayers as he is performing the behavior and just before any other cues. Gradually fade any old cues.

To make the trick Say Your Prayers go smoothly and to prevent your dog from scaring himself, choose a low stool that he can put his paws up on easily but that won't slide across the floor when he leans on it. Consider doing this trick on a rug or putting nonskid material under the legs of the stool.

Family Tricks

As your dog's handler, you are her connection to the human world. If your dog is part of a larger family, however, each member of the family needs to have a good working relationship with your dog. Start training your dog as an active participant in family life. Everyone will benefit from it.

Go Wake Up Daddy

What better way to wake up each morning than with a canine alarm clock? This trick requires a kiss or a nudge to the person the dog is waking up. You'll need a helper to act as the person the dog is supposed to rouse. Here are the shaping steps:

1. Start with the helper lying face down with his head on his folded arms. Have your helper hide a handful of lures under his arm and encourage your dog to investigate. When your dog goes to stick her nose under the helper's arm, click and treat.

2. Fade the lures in the helper's hand until the dog is nudging the person without the food being present. Click and treat any attempt to burrow under the person's arm.

3. Label the behavior Wake Up and the person's name just before the dog burrows under the person's arm.

4. Send your dog from gradually increasing distances until she is eagerly performing Wake Up from a room or two away.

5. Change helpers so that each member of the family gets a turn to be awakened by the dog.

6. Practice every Saturday morning to make sure no one misses out on breakfast!

As your dog begins to understand the concept of going and waking someone up, you can start to teach her to wake up specific people by having the person call her after you give the Wake Up command. You can wean your dog off this later when she begins to catch on.

Go Get Mom

This is a useful trick for kids and parents alike; for this trick the dog must go to a family member and lead them back to the person that sent them. What better way to round up the family for dinnertime then to send the dog to bring each member to the table?

1. Using the person your dog is going to get as your helper, call the dog back and forth between you and click and treat him for going to each person.

2. When your dog is doing this enthusiastically, label the behavior Go and the person's name right before the person calls the dog to Come.

3. Gradually move the people further apart so that the dog is going to the person from different rooms and up and down the stairs.

4. Replace the Come command with Go by saying Go Get Mom right before Mom calls the dog to come. The person the dog is searching for should be doing the clicking and treating when the dog finds them.

5. Once the dog starts to offer the behavior readily, he can be weaned off the clicker and treats, but he should still be acknowledged with praise and affection.

Supersmart Tricks

You learned earlier that dogs can be trained to perform any task that they are physically capable of doing. That said, the critical factor to successfully performing these tricks is your patience in handling your dog. Using your tools (see Chapter 4) and chain methods (see Chapter 7), start training your dog for these actions when you see that he is ready.

Dancing Dog

This trick is adorable but difficult for most dogs. To perform this trick the dog must balance on his hind legs and walk. You'll want to practice in short sessions to help your dog build up his back and leg muscles gradually. Be sure to work on a nonskid surface so that your dog does not injure himself. The shaping steps for teaching Dancing Dog are as follows:

1. With your dog in a Sit, hold your hand slightly above his nose and click and treat any effort to raise himself up on his back legs to touch your hand.
2. Raise your hand higher and continue to click and treat your dog for using his hind end to raise himself up and touch your hand.
3. Get your dog to hold the position longer by delaying the click by a second or two.
4. Gradually increase the time to several seconds.
5. Move your hand around and click and treat him for walking on his hind legs to touch it.
6. Turn your hand in a circle and click and treat your dog for walking on his hind legs to follow it.
7. Add the cue Dance by saying it just before the dog starts the behavior.

Ring a Bell

This trick involves teaching your dog to ring a bell with his nose or a paw. This trick is also quite practical, as you can teach your dog to ring a bell when he wants to go outside to the bathroom.

Hang a set of bells next to the door that you normally use to let your dog outside. Once he learns how to ring the bell with his mouth or nose, start having him do this each time he goes out to go potty. Pretty soon your dog will ring the bell to let you know he wants to go out. You may want to use a set of sleigh bells for this trick; four or five bells on a long strap may make it easier for your dog to learn to ring a bell, because it will give him more opportunities to be right.

The shaping steps for teaching your dog to Ring a Bell are as follows:

1. Put the bells on the floor and click and treat your dog for sniffing them. (You can use a Touch command if he knows one.)
2. Delay the click and wait for him to touch harder or mouth them before you click and treat.
3. Work at this until he's ringing the bells with purpose.
4. Hang the bells next to the door and repeat the above steps until he is ringing them reliably.
5. Gradually increase the distance he must travel to touch the bells.
6. Verbally label ringing the bells, Bells.

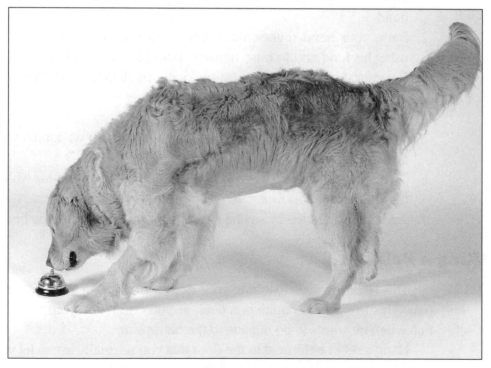

Use this trick to help your dog let you know when he needs to go out.

Get Me a Bottle of Water

This amazing trick involves your dog opening the refrigerator, taking out a bottle of water, closing the door, and bringing the bottle of water to you. You'll probably want to start with a water bottle and change the water bottle to a can of soda or a bottle of juice as your dog refines his techniques. This trick has three different parts: retrieving the bottle, opening the refrigerator door, and closing the refrigerator door.

Retrieving the Water Bottle

1. Hand your dog a bottle of water and tell him to Take It. Click and treat your dog for hanging on to it for several seconds at a time.
2. Move away from your dog and have him come to you over greater and greater distances. Click and treat him first as he is moving to you and then for delivering the bottle to your hand.
3. Place the bottle on the floor and tell your dog to Take It, then Bring It. Click and treat him for retrieving it, then gradually withhold the click until the dog is on his way back to you.
4. Put the bottle on a low shelf of the refrigerator and practice having the dog Take It. Click and treat your dog for at first approaching, then taking, then bringing the bottle to you over short training sessions.

Opening the Refrigerator Door

1. Put a strap on the refrigerator door to make it easier for your dog to open it.
2. Starting with the refrigerator door open, hand your dog the strap and tell him Take It. Click and treat him for taking the strap.
3. Once your dog is taking the strap easily, delay the click for an extra second or two and click and treat your dog for holding it.
4. Standing slightly behind your dog, call him back to you while he holds the strap. You may need to go back and teach your dog the formal retrieve (see Chapter 7) with the strap or at least review it with him.
5. When your dog can hold onto the strap while backing up, click and treat him for actually moving the door.

6. Gradually close the door until it's almost clicked shut so that your dog has to pull harder to open it.

7. Once your dog can open the door when it's shut all the way, try letting him retrieve the strap on his own. At first, click and treat any attempt to take the strap.

8. Gradually add a little distance so that your dog is approaching the refrigerator from greater and greater distances.

9. Eventually delay your click so that your dog is taking the strap and starting to back up to pull the door open before you click. If at any time he seems confused and the behavior falls apart, go back and break things down into smaller parts and gradually rebuild the behavior.

10. Once the dog is grabbing the strap when you point to it, go ahead and label the behavior Drink right before the dog reaches for the strap. Later, the label/cue might become Go Get Me a Drink, but in the beginning your dog will pay attention to the one-word cue Drink.

Closing the Refrigerator Door (dog uses his nose)

1. Once your dog is comfortable holding the bottle in his mouth, practice having him target the refrigerator door with his nose.

2. Open the door a little, give a Touch command, and click and treat him for moving the door shut even a little.

3. Gradually leave the door open a little more until the dog is shutting the door with purpose. Make sure you click and treat your dog for even small attempts to push the door shut.

4. Verbally label the behavior Shut the Door.

Close the Door (dog uses his paws)

1. Use a paw target to get your dog to touch the refrigerator with his paws, then click and treat.

2. Open the door a little and tell your dog to paw the door; click and treat him for moving the door shut.

3. Gradually open the door more so your dog has to push the door harder to earn the click and treat.

4. Verbally label the behavior Shut the Door.

Review each piece to put them all together. Open the refrigerator door (keep the bottle on a lower shelf), and have your dog take the bottle. When he still has the bottle in his mouth, call him around the door and tell him to push it shut. Practice these two steps until they are fluid. Then add the command to Take It (the door strap), followed by retrieving the bottle. Practice these together until they are fluid. Then, combine them with closing the door. You may have to go back and forth a bit to keep each part of the behavior strong until eventually it is one continuous behavior.

ALERT!

Be careful what item you choose for your dog to retrieve. Water bottles are the easiest for the dog to grasp at first, and later you can work up to retrieving cans or glass. If you have a dog that tends to bite down hard when he retrieves things, you may want to practice with empty cans first to prevent him from scaring himself or making a mess of your kitchen.

Go Left, Go Right

Teaching your dog how to distinguish from his left and right will amaze your friends and family. It will also enable you to direct your dog to exactly where you want him to go.

1. Start with your dog in front of an object (like a chair) and put a target lid about three feet to the left of it.
2. Send your dog to go Touch, and click and treat him for responding.
3. Repeat this at gradually increasing distances, clicking right before your dog touches his nose to the target.
4. When your dog is offering the behavior readily, say the new cue Go Left just before he is about to move forward to touch the target. Repeat this until he will go to the left when you say left.
5. Fade the target by making it smaller (use scissors to cut it into smaller pieces) until your dog simply moves left on command.
6. To teach your dog to Go Right, simply follow all the same steps except with everything on the right.

You can combine the Go Left and Go Right commands with retrieving tricks by lining up several objects in a row and asking your dog to take the one on the left or the right. If nothing else, this trick will give you a better foundation for teaching your dog more complicated tricks.

Find It

Sending your dog to find something you have lost is useful and exciting to the dog. Losing your wallet or keys in a pile of leaves or along your walking route could be disastrous—unless your dog can help in the search.

1. Choose an item with lots of your scent on it (like a hat or a hair tie) and show it to your dog.
2. Have someone hold your dog's collar while you hide the item somewhere obvious at first.
3. Release your dog to go find it and click and treat him as he approaches it.
4. Gradually increase the difficulty by hiding it in more challenging places.
5. Find another item to practice with and try again.
6. Label the behavior Find It as the dog moves toward the object.

Multi-Dog Tricks

Successful multi-dog tricks require that each dog understands the behavior and can perform it on a reliable cue. Before attempting it with more than one dog, go over the steps with each dog individually. If things fall apart or don't go as well as planned, review the steps with each dog separately.

These tricks are meant to be performed by two or three dogs at once. You may want to enlist the help of multiple handlers, one for each dog. The helpers' roles will be to reinforce and reward individual dogs for performing correctly while they get used to performing tricks as a team.

Double-Dog Roll Over

This trick involves two dogs rolling over at the same time. As you position the dogs, make sure you leave enough space in between them so that they don't crash into each other. Another way you could perform this trick would be to have the dogs roll over one at a time, one right after the other. Shaping steps for the Double-Dog Roll Over are as follows:

1. Have each dog lie about three feet apart. Allow more space if the dogs are giant breeds.
2. Reinforce each dog for holding the Down/Stay position.
3. Cue the dogs to Roll Over one at a time (reinforce the others for staying until they have been cued), or give the cue for all the dogs to roll at the same time.
4. Experiment with giving a cue to each dog and then giving one cue to the group and see which version of the trick looks flashier.
5. If you are cueing all the dogs at once, you need only one click for all of them, but treat each dog with her own cookie.
6. If you are cueing each dog separately, click and treat that dog before asking the next one to go.
7. Once the dogs are performing reliably, verbally label the behavior Everybody Over, or label each individual rollover with the dog's name and then the Roll Over command.

Pass the Cookie Please

This trick requires two dogs, one sitting in front of the other. The first dog balances a cookie on her nose and on cue, tosses her head back, flinging the cookie over her head to the dog sitting behind her. The dog sitting behind her catches it and eats it as her reward. Review the steps for the Balance a Cookie on Your Nose trick on page 99.

Flipping over the head is easier for most dogs to master (especially with a larger cookie) than flipping and catching. After five repetitions, click and treat the dog only for flipping the cookie over his head, not into his own mouth. Here are the shaping steps:

1. Start with a cookie that is too big for the flipper dog to eat in one bite.
2. Once the dog is balancing the cookie easily, label this stay.
3. Release him with Okay and click the movement of the head.
4. Reward him with a small treat.
5. Replace the cookie and begin again.
6. After 5 repetitions, withhold your click until he gives a larger movement or a more defined toss of the cookie. It is important to observe him closely and click the bigger tosses and ignore the smaller ones.
7. Use a higher level treat like cheese or chicken so he is less likely to dive on the cookie and starts working harder to earn the click and the high-end reward that you control.

FACT

It requires good timing of the click to get your dog to understand that it's the toss of her head that you are looking for. Most dogs will toss their heads back to get the cookie off their noses. Some will even flip it and catch it if you practice enough. It's important that you let your dog develop her own style by practicing frequently.

Add the second dog to the mix once your cookie-balancing dog has a good toss and is no longer immediately pursuing the dropped cookie. Practice having the second dog catch the cookie after the first dog tosses it. This may require lots of practice to get the timing and coordination just right.

The commands or labels will be Hold It, Stay, and then Okay, which will cause the dog holding the cookie to toss the cookie. Be sure you click and treat the first dog for not pursuing the tossed cookie. You can ask another person to help you and have them click and treat the first dog for staying in place. It's a good idea to have your helper put a leash on the first dog and step on it so that he has more opportunities to be right.

Everybody Wave

This adorable trick can be performed with any number of dogs. The dogs should line up facing their audience and raise their paws in the air as if waving hello. The shaping steps for teaching a group of dogs to wave are as follows:

1. Make sure each dog can fluidly and reliably Wave on a hand signal.
2. Line the dogs up and reinforce them for holding a Stay.
3. Cue the dogs to Wave and click and treat all of them.
4. Practice with two dogs at a time until they are competing with each other to raise their paws the fastest.
5. Encourage extra-fast efforts by clicking and treating only the dog that was first.
6. Gradually add more dogs, following the same rules; the faster dogs get treated more often than the slower dogs.
7. If one dog is particularly slow, take her aside and teach her to Wave faster before putting her back into the group.

When having a group of dogs perform together, you might like to stagger the behaviors so that the dogs perform them one after the other. Initially, you may want to use a helper to reinforce the dogs that are waiting for their turns.

This trick is an adorable way to say hello or good-bye during a visit with schoolchildren or at a nursing home. You can vary how you have the dogs perform it by having them wave individually or as a group. You can also improve on each dog's individual wave by only clicking and treating the best versions of the wave, one aspect at a time. For instance, you might improve the speed of the dog's response by giving the cue and only clicking and treating when he offers the behavior within a certain amount of time (say three seconds). You might improve the height of the wave by only clicking and treating the higher waves and ignoring the lower ones, telling the dog to try again. Just be sure that you are concentrating on one aspect at a time so as not to confuse the dog.

Leap Frog

Be careful which dogs you choose for this trick; not all dogs are comfortable having other dogs jump over them. This trick requires two or three dogs. While the rest of the dogs lie down about three feet apart, the third dog leaps over their backs and lies down next to the last dog. The first dog then repeats this, and so on.

1. Reinforce all the dogs for lying down and holding the Down/Stay.
2. Work the first dog by having her touch her nose to the target stick held over the back of the first dog. Use the target stick to help her hop over the other dogs one at a time; click and treat each hop.
3. When the last dog has been hopped over, have her lie down and let the next dog go.
4. Reinforce the other dogs for holding the Down/Stay position. You may need a helper for this.
5. To increase your dog's tolerance for being hopped over, practice reinforcing your dog for letting you step over her.
6. Adding speed to this trick will make it impressive and flashy; just be sure to build up to it slowly and don't rush the dogs. They will move faster when they are comfortable.

The dog lying down should have a reliable Down/Stay so as not to scare the dog being taught to jump over him.

If you are going to train multiple dogs to work together, it's a good idea to make sure they get along well and are not competitive over food. Each dog should be taught how to perform the behavior separately until the trick is on a reliable cue before being asked to perform it in a group.

Take a Bow

For this trick, the dog brings her front end close to the ground, with her chest resting on the floor, lifts her tail end in the air, and holds the position. You can have the dogs do it all at the same time or one after the other.

1. It's probably best to start with all the dogs in the Sit/Stay position. Reinforce each dog for holding the Stay.
2. Give the cue for Bow to all the dogs at once, or each dog individually. Click and treat those dogs that perform the behavior correctly.
3. Continue to practice until all the dogs are performing in unison. Don't be afraid to go back and review the steps with each dog individually if the trick starts to fall apart. (See Chapter 6 for the shaping steps for teaching your dog to bow.)

It can't be stressed enough that if you don't reward the dogs that are waiting their turn to perform, you will lose their interest. Rewarding the dogs that are waiting will ensure that all the dogs stay focused and ready to work.

Walking the Dog

This trick involves two dogs. One dog wears a collar and leash and the other dog carries the leash in her mouth.

1. Teach your dog to retrieve and carry a leash. (See Chapter 7 for shaping the retrieve behavior.)
2. Once your dog is retrieving the leash easily, start practicing having her hold it with some resistance. (Hold on to the end and give a little tug.)

3. Hand your dog the leash and click and treat her for grabbing it and walking with you.
4. With the leash firmly in your dog's mouth, practice giving it a tug, and click and treat her for pulling back or hanging on.
5. Gradually increase the amount of resistance you offer to prepare your dog for a real dog on the end of the leash.
6. When your dog can carry the leash while you are offering resistance, then add a real dog. (The dog you add should be an adult with some leash manners, and the leash should be attached to a flat buckled collar.)
7. Click and treat the dog being led for walking slightly ahead of the other dog but not outright pulling.

Tips for a Better Performance

When working with multiple dogs, it quickly becomes apparent that the better able the dogs are to perform the tricks alone, the more likely they are to cooperate as a group. Here are some tricks to working with groups of dogs that understand the basic trick but need to learn how to do the behavior in unison:

Building duration into the behavior makes a cute trick even more impressive.

- Only treat those dogs that perform the trick fast.
- Point to the individual dog that you are working with as you give the cue.

- Use a helper to reward the other dogs for holding a Stay while you work with an individual dog.
- Review tricks regularly with each individual dog to keep performance consistent.
- Vary the quality and quantity of treats to keep your dog guessing and trying harder to earn the next goodie.
- Keep your sessions short and frequent to keep the dogs focused and sharp.

The show-off in every dog is something to celebrate! Let your dog— or dogs—indulge his sense of humor and excitement by making him part of your entertainment committee. Enjoy spending time teaching your dog tricks and performing them for friends and family. Developing a healthy training relationship with your dog will make it easier to communicate with him and help you gain control of behavior problems.

CHAPTER 9

Techniques and Tools for Problem Solving

If you don't train your dog or provide any structure, you will be rewarded with a dog that behaves exactly as you taught her to behave: in ways that are out of control, demanding, mischievous, and destructive. Invest the time, patience, and love to get your dog off to a good start, and you will have a companion that enhances your family's life.

9

Set the Best Environment

Living with a dog need not be complicated, but with the changing demands of life in our world, dogs are left to cope with an amazing amount of stress and changes that their ancestors never encountered. To say that our full schedules are going to change dramatically when we take on a dog as a member of our family is unrealistic; however, we must make accommodations for them and be sure we meet their needs. If we are unable or unwilling to spend more time at home with our pets, we must be willing to hire someone to take care of their needs for us.

Dogs are pack animals that were meant to live in groups; they are not solitary animals and do not enjoy spending hours alone for days at a time. The root of many dogs' behavior problems lies in a lack of stimulation and energy outlets. Most people can't just quit their jobs to stay at home with their dogs, but the emergence of quality doggie day care programs, reputable pet sitters, and dog parks has made it possible to incorporate taking care of a dog into a busy life.

QUESTION?

Who will exercise your dog if you can't?
For many dogs, having a dog walker to play with in the middle of the day, or spending a day at a doggie day care center, is not a frivolous luxury; it's necessary exercise and social time with other dogs and people.

Behavior problems in dogs lead many people to seek help from a dog trainer or attend a group training class. Problems usually range from jumping or mouthing to excessive barking and aggression. If you visit an animal shelter, you will see many dogs between the ages of nine months and two years whose families simply didn't have time for their energy and antics. Behavior problems don't have to end at an animal shelter if you understand a little about how dogs think and what motivates them to do what they do.

When you take a dog into your home, you must make room for him. Dogs require a lot of love and training and care, but they give so much more back in loyalty and love. Be sure to give your dog the best home you possibly can. You will be rewarded a hundred fold. If your dog's behavior is less than ideal, don't give up on him. All dogs, no matter how sweet and compliant they are, need training, limits, exercise, and house rules.

Analyze the Problem

When it comes to trying to solve a dog's behavior problem, people often think too much. They blame the dog for going potty on the carpet out of spite when in reality the dog isn't being walked enough! Let's be clear: Dogs don't hold grudges, they don't do things out of spite, and they are not sorry for anything. Dogs are not capable of those thoughts. They live in the moment, they are opportunistic, and they repeat behavior that is reinforced, even if it's reinforced negatively.

Close supervision and management are the keys to fixing behavior problems.

Dogs are animals, and animals do things that sometimes baffle humans, despite our best attempts to understand them. To solve an existing behavior problem, it is crucial to sit down with your family members and figure out the details of the problem. Using the following questions as a guide, try to identify and define what the dog is actually doing, when she is doing it, and what you might be able to teach her to do instead.

- **Problem.** What does the dog actually do? Write it down and describe it in as much detail as possible.
- **Cause.** What triggers this behavior? Is it the presence of a strange dog, the doorbell, or a new person?

- **Frequency.** How often does the dog do the behavior? Once a minute, nonstop, every time the trigger is present, or only half the time it is present?
- **Consequence.** What has been done to stop the behavior? What consequence results when the dog responds to the trigger?
- **Reinforcement history.** How long has the dog been doing the behavior and what about it is reinforcing him to repeat it?
- **Management.** What can you do to prevent the dog from practicing the behavior while you are retraining him?

By identifying the actual source of the problem, you will be able to develop a plan for retraining the dog to respond in a more appropriate way. Let everyone who takes care of the dog participate in the exercise, as well as future training sessions.

Most dog owners know exactly what they want their dogs to stop doing, but very few have put thought into what the dog should do instead. Unless you develop a plan for an acceptable alternative, you will not get rid of problem behavior.

Behavior Management

Prevention isn't training, but it can help you get rid of unwanted behavior, because you are not allowing the dog to practice it repeatedly. "Management" involves putting the dog in a separate room or crate when visitors come or stepping on the leash to prevent the dog from jumping. The less the dog gets to practice the wrong behavior, the less you will have to do to convince him that the right behavior is more rewarding and desirable. Behavior management does not mean correcting, reprimanding, or punishing your dog.

Some people manage their dog's behavior with crates, gates, and pens; others use leashes or time outs. It doesn't matter how you manage your dog's behavior, as long as it keeps your dog from practicing the wrong behavior over and over. You want to change problem behavior, and management prevents the dog from rewarding himself. Consider these behavior management ideas:

- Use a crate when you can't watch your dog if he is a destructive chewer.
- Keep a leash on your dog when company visits, and put your foot on it to prevent jumping.
- Don't allow your dog off leash in public places if he doesn't come when he's called.
- Avoid other dogs if your dog is aggressive around them.
- If your dog likes to escape out the front door, deny access to it.
- If your dog likes to bite the mailman, don't tie him outside the front door.
- If your dog is not fully housebroken, don't allow him unsupervised freedom.

Even adolescent dogs need a nap time in a safe place.

Management and prevention keep a behavior problem from perpetuating itself; use them while you are retraining your dog to do something more appropriate. Prevention is not a 100 percent solution, but it can help you move toward your goal by not reinforcing any inappropriate behavior.

Alternate Behavior

You've gotten to the root of the bad behavior, and you have an interim plan in place—management. The next step is understanding reinforcement and replacement behavior. You need to provide reinforcement for a desirable behavior to replace the behavior you don't like. Otherwise, the dog will revert back to the old behavior. Think about reinforcing a behavior that is easy to teach and easy for the dog to perform, even with a lot of distractions.

What Reinforces the Wrong Behavior?

Look closely at the circumstances surrounding the misbehavior and see what the dog finds reinforcing about it. If he jumps and people yell at him and shove him off, perhaps he likes the attention and they should ignore him instead. Maybe there is a member of your household that encourages the dog to jump and isn't consistent about reinforcing the dog for sitting instead.

By removing the source of the reinforcement, you can put a good dent in getting rid of a behavior problem. In many cases, the dog is getting way too much attention for the wrong behavior and needs more information about what is going right. If there isn't anything going right, then the dog has too much freedom and too many options. In this case, you'll need to rethink your training program and make it easier for your dog to be right.

Providing an undesirable consequence for a behavior, such as turning away from a barking dog, is very effective in changing the behavior. Being ignored was not the outcome the dog expected; by ignoring him you are saying that barking doesn't work.

Reinforcing the Right Behavior

To change a behavior that has become a habit, you need to provide a high rate of reinforcement for the appropriate behavior or it will never occur to the dog to try anything else. Dogs do what works, so if they get attention for the wrong behavior, they are likely to repeat it in the future. If they are reinforced for a more appropriate behavior with really yummy treats or exciting games of fetch, they will tend to make the good things happen again by repeating the behavior.

Every reinforcement for the right behavior is like money in the bank. If your dog's bank account for the undesirable behavior is high, you will need to build up a considerable history of reinforcement of the alternate behavior. Practice often, give occasional jackpots (a handful of small goodies or an extra-long game of fetch or tug), and set your dog up to succeed.

Training an Incompatible Behavior

Teaching the dog an acceptable behavior solves many behavior problems because a dog can't necessarily do two things at once. For instance, a dog can't sit politely to greet a stranger and jump on her at the same time. Giving the dog an alternate behavior gives you more control over her, and it also allows you to reward her for an appropriate response. Perhaps your dog could:

A Bow may be a better way to greet a guest rather than jumping on them.

- Greet visitors with a toy in her mouth instead of jumping on them.
- Go to her bed or mat when the doorbell rings.
- Do a play Bow when she sees another dog.
- Retrieve a toy instead of barking at the window at a passersby.

- Look at you instead of lunging at other dogs.
- Target your hand (see Chapter 4) instead of running away.

Use this opportunity to be creative, and find solutions that suit your needs and your dog's natural inclinations. Think of this as another way you're making it easy for training to be successful.

Problem-Solving Tools

Every dog owner needs to be armed with tools and tricks to teach his dog how to live with people in a safe, relaxed manner. Knowing your dog—his energy level, his tolerance of other dogs, his likes and dislikes—will be a huge asset in training him to respond to you in appropriate ways.

Map out the changes to your dog's routine that you have decided to implement, and determine a time frame for training him. Set up a schedule of consistent practice times so you teach each part of each behavior in small digestible portions, to be built upon each time you work your dog. Make sure you also consider the whole dog, mind and body, and provide for all of your dog's needs.

ALERT!

The most reliable outcome of punishment is a breakdown of the relationship and the trust that we have worked so hard to cultivate. Punishment doesn't change behavior permanently unless there is incentive to do something else.

Exercise

Don't let this get by you. Playing, running, fetching, and having time with you is crucial to a dog's sanity. Be sure that your dog gets at least thirty to sixty minutes a day of all-out running or playtime with other dogs before you even consider training him to be a better companion. If your dog has tons of toys but only plays with a few, consider grouping them in sets of ten and rotating them each week to keep things interesting. Make a play date with your neighbor's dog, sign up for doggie day care, or hire a pet sitter to exercise your dog while you're at work so that you can concentrate on training your dog and have a willing student who is ready to work.

Regular exercise is important to overall behavior management.

Basic Obedience

Nothing beats the companionship of a well-trained dog. A dog that responds to Sit, Down, and Come can be taken many places and not put you to shame. Spend time teaching these basics, at first in an environment with only a few distractions and then build up to being able to work somewhere outdoors or around other dogs.

Teaching your dog to Sit, Lie Down, and Come is useful and can replace unwanted behavior. For your dog's training to be effective, you must practice often, and the dog's response to commands must not be dependent on the environment or the presence of food. Weaning your dog off of food lures and lots of extra commands and prompting will make you both relaxed in public, because you know what to expect from each other.

If your dog's response to commands around distractions falls apart, it simply means you have more training to do. Manipulating the variables slowly to maintain your dog's response to commands is one key to success.

If you work at it, it won't be long before you are rewarded with an obedient dog that you can take anywhere.

Consider taking a group class. The distraction of other dogs will help your dog realize that he must learn to pay attention to you. Try to make sure the ratio of teacher to student is high; twelve students to two instructors is ideal.

Choose to Sit

Dogs don't learn self-control unless they are allowed to make choices and are rewarded for making good ones. Using a clicker and treats to mark and reward behavior is critical. The clicker allows you to mark the right choice and begin a bank account for the right behavior. The following exercise, Choose to Sit, is one example of helping your dog learn self-control.

1. Greet visitors with the dog on a leash.
2. If the dog jumps, the visitor goes away.
3. If the dog sits, the visitor stays and the handler clicks and treats.
4. The dog learns by trial and error how to get the person to pay attention to him.
5. The handler supplies information by clicking and treating the right responses.
6. The visitor supplies consequences for not sitting by not allowing the dog to say hello to her.

Label the behavior Sit right before the dog's bottom hits the floor. In reality, this behavior does not need a label since we are using an environmental cue (the presence of a person) to trigger the behavior of sitting. Most people nag their dogs too much and repeat sit, sit, SIT while the dog jumps all over some poor visitor. Teaching greeting behavior this way gives the responsibility to the dog, who will learn that visitor = sit = reward.

As you try to solve your dog's behavior problems, keep this example in mind. Learning will last longer when the dog figures out on his own what the rewardable behavior is, especially if the dog is usually excellent in the absence of distractions but falls apart in public.

Attention Game

The next exercise is another self-control exercise that helps your dog figure out how to pay attention to you. The Attention Game is intended to teach your dog to check in with you often and to ignore distractions. In time, teaching your dog to check in with you will give him a greater awareness of you, which will improve his recall and heeling commands. Dogs who have some responsibility to know where you are will not stray far away when they are off their leashes. They will check in often and come back easily when you call because they know you are in control. Here's how the game works:

1. In a quiet room, sit in a chair with your dog on a leash.
2. Ignore your dog until he looks in your direction, then click and treat.
3. Ignore him again until he looks back at you, then click and treat.
4. Time yourself for one minute and count how many times he looks at you in that minute. If your dog looks at you six or more times in a minute, you are ready to add distractions. Change locations by working alone in the kitchen, then with a person in the room. Go outside at different times of day. Add a small pile of food 10 feet away from the dog, a person bouncing a ball, or another dog 20 feet away.
5. Repeat this again in a new place or with a distraction and repeat the one-minute test. The distraction is too intense if your dog looks at you less than twice a minute.
6. Repeat this until your dog is looking at you six or more times a minute and then change the distraction again.
7. If your dog doesn't look at you more than twice in a minute for several repetitions, you will probably need to move away from the distraction or go somewhere less distracting.

8. Increase the quality and quantity of the rewards every once in a while to intensify the dog's response and increase the likelihood that he will look at you more often.

9. Jackpot exceptional behavior. If your dog ignores an unexpected distraction, be sure to reward him with a whole handful of goodies to reinforce the good performance.

Teaching your dog to Leave It is an essential skill for teaching self control.

Your goal with this game is to increase your dog's attention to you. As a result of paying attention to you, your dog is learning to block out distractions and maintain self-control.

Having techniques and tools to help you teach your dog what is expected of him will make your training sessions run smoothly, and it will also make solving behavior problems that much more productive. Behavior problems need not be mysterious, and they certainly should not be the reason to surrender a dog to an animal shelter. With a little knowledge and skill, you can teach your dog to be a well-behaved member of your family.

CHAPTER 10

A Word about Punishment

As humans, we are absolutely convinced that to change behavior we must provide some sort of punishment that will eliminate bad behavior altogether. In truth, no animals, including humans, respond well to punishment. Although it has been part of training dogs for decades, punishment is not a good or effective way to train a well-behaved family pet.

Punishment Can Make Things Worse

Over time, many trainers have found that it is totally unnecessary to use punishment to get reliable, acceptable behavior. In many cases, using punishment can actually make problems worse. Consider these two points:

- Punishment stops behavior, but it does not teach or provide another choice.
- The many negative side effects of punishment outweigh the short-term benefits.

The best human example of the ineffectiveness of punishment is a speeding ticket. If you've ever been pulled over for speeding, you'll understand. The moment the lights flash behind you is horrible. When you're actually pulled over, your heart races, you stutter and stammer, and you wait and wait and wait. You end up with a fine to pay and points on your insurance. Do you stop speeding? Well, maybe for a little while. But one day when you're running late, you speed again, and you get away with it.

Management tools (see Chapter 9) will result in a well-behaved dog without the fallout of a deteriorated relationship and the breakdown of trust that most punishment causes. Management eliminates the opportunity for wrong behavior, making it easier for your dog to choose the right one.

You may have been a little more careful this time, avoiding speed traps and keeping your eyes open, but you were speeding. After being punished severely not long ago, how could you go back to that behavior? Quite simply, the punishment made you a better speeder! You are no longer a random, careless speeder; you actually look for cruisers and avoid known speed traps. The punishment actually improved the way you speed.

Punishment Is Reactive

The first problem with punishment is that it is a response to bad behavior, whereas training initiates good behavior. The second problem with punishment as a training tool is that you can't always control what the student learns. In fact, punishment puts the subject in an excitable and defensive emotional state, which interferes with the dog's ability to learn anything.

Another reason that punishment is not very effective for fixing behavior problems is that it is only part of the equation. Punishment only stops the unwanted behavior; it does not show the dog what he should have done instead. Punishment occurs too late to teach anything because by the time it is delivered, the dog has already done the undesirable behavior and cannot undo it.

Punishing your dog for jumping on the company will not make him want to sit in front of them next time. In fact, punishment delivered by a visitor or in the presence of one might actually teach your dog to be fearful of

Finding the motivation for barking is essential to redirecting it.

visitors; it teaches him it can be unpleasant to be around strangers. This is not what you want. After working so hard to make sure your dog is social with people, it would be detrimental to all to start punishing him for being friendly.

Timing Is Everything

If you are going to use punishment and have it mean anything, the timing of the correction has to be precise; it must happen the moment the undesirable behavior begins. Not many people are capable of doing this. Another issue with the timing of the correction is that the dog is probably overstimulated and excited, which means her brain is not in learning mode. To process information, a dog has to be in a fairly relaxed state.

Instead of punishing your dog for bad behavior, you can offer her a reward for stopping the behavior. Again, the timing has to be just right. The dog would need to be rewarded as soon as the inappropriate behavior stopped. The timing of the reward here is the instructive part for the dog. If the behavior you are trying to fix is one the dog has been practicing for a long time, a very high rate of reinforcement for the right behavior must be employed or the new desirable behavior will not replace the old behavior. Remember that old habits die hard, and it is difficult to adopt new ways of doing things without it being heavily reinforced for the right choices. Once your dog is overexcited, she can't learn anything. Her behavior will either get more frantic or she will shut down completely. The person delivering the punishment is likely to add more punishment, continuing the unproductive cycle, and no real learning happens.

Redirect the Behavior

Rather than using corrections (a polite word for "punishment), either redirect or interrupt the dog before he starts the behavior. At the first sign of undesirable behavior, the dog must be interrupted and redirected to a more appropriate behavior. An interruption could be something like saying the dog's name, or touching the dog on the shoulder, or turning away from whatever captured his interest. Pay attention to your dog's levels of distraction and excitement. Overstimulation will prevent him from learning anything. Build up to working around intense distractions rather than jumping into chaos and hoping for the best.

To work effectively, interruptions must be delivered before the dog starts the behavior. In the case of barking, for instance, if you wait until the dog is barking and frantic you will not be able to distract him from what he's barking at in order to teach him anything. For a dog with a one-track mind, you could use a strong correction and it still wouldn't phase him or stop his behavior. It would be like trying to reason with someone who is angry. A person not in a rational frame of mind is not capable of listening to you or being reasonable.

Instead, start paying attention to what triggers the barking, and interrupt the dog while he's still thinking about it. To short-circuit an undesirable behavior, you might have the dog go to his bed or move further away from the distractions so he's not as excited. Your goal is to interrupt him close to the distractions, but it is unreasonable to try to train him there in the beginning. As with any constructive and lasting training, you need to start with small, simple steps that enable the dog to be successful.

Providing appropriate things to chew on is essential to prevent destructive chewing.

Establishing New Patterns

Two basic things are required to stop unwanted behavior and get your dog to develop a new pattern of behavior. First, you must have a set plan to accomplish your goal. Second, you must prevent the dog from practicing the old behavior while you are retraining her. Setting up a new pattern of behavior isn't easy for dogs. Just like humans, once they get into a habit, they tend to do things the same way again and again if we let them.

Repetition

The important thing to remember when changing a pattern is that you need to practice the new pattern over and over and reward the dog repeatedly for the new behavior until she adopts it as her own. In the meantime, if you want to get where you are going faster, you need to stop allowing the dog to reinforce herself for the wrong behavior by preventing it from happening. Stepping on the leash to prevent jumping will not, by itself, teach your dog to sit, but it will reduce her options and make sitting more likely, because that is the only behavior getting rewarded.

An Ounce of Prevention

The more time you spend with dogs, the more you will find that a large part of training is really management. Gates, crates, and pens can be your best friends when raising and training a dog. Although they don't teach the dog not to chew the couch or pee on the carpet, they prevent inappropriate behaviors from becoming bad habits. Managing a dog's environment helps him to be right by limiting his choices. It isn't the solution to all of your behavior problems, but it is an integral part of it.

As you figure out a plan for what you want your dog to do, it's important to write it out and keep track of it. Make sure any treats, clicker, or other equipment are conveniently located in your house or yard, allowing you to reward your dog whenever the opportunity arises. If the alternate behavior is complicated, break it down into steps and practice with your dog frequently.

For example, a fence is a management tool for dogs that enjoy playing in their yards and owners who want to keep them there. A baby gate in the kitchen limits the dog's freedom so that he can't get into trouble in the rest of the house. When you don't have time to teach your dog to sit for a guest, putting your dog behind a gate would be a better way to manage his jumping problem than letting him dive onto a visitor or run out the front door.

The Fallout of Punishment: Aggression

If punishment is mistimed or too severe, it can often cause the dog to turn and bite whoever is closest. Dogs that are corrected for barking and lunging at people or other dogs don't learn to like them; in fact, many of these animals become more unpredictable and dangerous. They learn that the presence of other dogs or people means they are about to be punished, so they will often bite without warning.

When you pay attention to what's going right and ignore what the dog is doing wrong, you'll begin to reap the rewards. Dogs are social creatures that crave attention, so even negative attention when they are misbehaving may be encouragement enough to repeat the very behavior you are trying so hard to eliminate.

Warnings Work for a Reason

If you physically punish a dog for growling, he may stop growling and skip right to the bite instead. You have made that dog far more dangerous because he no longer warns people that he is not comfortable, he just bites them. You have, in essence, created a better biter. Growling is a dog's way of warning us that he is uncomfortable and that if the person or dog doesn't go away there's going to be trouble. Punishing the warning doesn't make sense; we want to change the way the dog feels about the person or dog, not take away the warning that he is about to bite. This is nature's way of letting us know we have a problem, and it gives us time to do something about it before the dog bites.

Training Versus Punishment

Never use punishment with any problem related to aggression around people or dogs. The risk of creating a better biter is just too high. Here are five reasons to teach your dog instead of punish him.

1. Punishment must be repeated frequently to remind the dog to avoid her mistake.
2. Punishment doesn't teach the dog anything; dogs with little confidence will wilt.
3. With punishment, you can't control what the dog learns.
4. Punishment can damage the relationship between owner and dog.
5. Punishment can accelerate aggression by suppressing all warning signs and teaching the dog to skip right to the bite.

There are many reasons for not using punishment in training your dog. In general, punishment misses the point. It comes too late to be instructive, and it has the danger of teaching the dog to be better at the very behavior we are trying to eliminate.

If your dog is behaving so poorly that you think she needs punishment, then the real problem is that she needs more information about what she has to do to be right. Instead of spending your time figuring out how to stop the behaviors you don't like, map out what you want the dog to do instead and retrain her.

FACT

Aggression and fearfulness are emotional states where the dog is in a fight-or-flight mode, not a learning mode. In this frame of mind, a dog is unable to learn anything. He must be comfortable, not defensive, to learn appropriate nonaggressive or nonfearful responses.

If a dog's basic needs for exercise, training, and attention are met and he is carefully managed according to her age and training level, you will have fewer behavioral problems and less to correct. Think carefully about how you use punishment, because behavioral problems often indicate a much larger issue. If you want a well-behaved dog that responds to you quickly and is fun to be around, don't use punishment to teach him; it won't get you where you want to go.

CHAPTER 11

Training a More Desirable Behavior

When dealing with behavior problems, it is essential that you plan out what your dog should do in place of the behavior you are trying to eliminate. If you want to change inappropriate behavior permanently, you must replace it with the right behavior and heavily reinforce it or no real change will occur.

Have a Plan

You must give your dog a clear task to perform in place of the behavior you want her to stop. If your dog has too many choices, she may choose incorrectly. This may leave you frustrated that she's not "getting it," which is unfair to both of you.

A trick your dog knows well can help keep her from jumping while greeting visitors.

To have a dog that is trained to be responsive and enjoyable, you will need to get your family's act together. The fastest way to change your dog's unwanted behavior is to stop reinforcing the incorrect behavior and start reinforcing an alternative behavior in its place. There are endless possibilities to choose from. Sit down with your family and review the behavior questions in Chapter 9. Then, come up with ideas on how you want your dog to respond in different situations. When choosing which behaviors to reinforce, you'll want to keep the following points in mind:

- Keep it simple.
- Choose something incompatible with the wrong behavior.

- Plan ahead and be prepared. Carry your treats and clicker with you.
- Control the variables, such as distractions and the environment.
- Avoid reinforcing the wrong behavior.
- Build a bank account for good behavior.
- Teach your dog to perform the desired behavior anywhere.

ALERT!

So often people know what they don't want a dog to do, but few people can define concisely what they want their dogs to do instead. Having a positively phrased goal will help you design a training plan that can be put to use right away.

Every time the dog gets to practice the old undesirable behavior she is putting money in the bank for doing that behavior again. Preventing the wrong behavior from happening is half of the training.

Keep It Simple

Whatever you choose as the alternate behavior should be simple for the dog to offer quickly and reliably. Choose a single behavior, such as Sit or Down, and reinforce it often. If the behavior is too complicated or involved, your dog may lose interest and go back to the undesirable behavior. A simple behavior like Sit is something you are likely to notice and reinforce even in a distracting environment. Be sure your dog knows the behavior well by applying the Ten in a Row rule.

Choose an Incompatible Behavior

Make sure that the new behavior is incompatible with the undesirable behavior. For instance, a dog cannot sit and jump at the same time. If you reinforce sitting as the desirable behavior when your dog greets new people, it won't be long before your dog doesn't even try to jump. Be forewarned: Replacing jumping with sitting takes lots of time and practice before the dog will offer it on her own. Practice in short, frequent sessions and as opportunities present themselves from day to day. Remember, preventing jumping as an option by putting your foot on the leash will help your dog to be right more often.

Plan Ahead for Success

If you want a well-trained dog that responds to your commands everywhere, you have to train her everywhere. Dogs pick things up quickly, but they are lousy generalizers. They tend to revert to old, ingrained behaviors in new environments. If you haven't taught your dog to sit when greeting strangers at the park, that will not be her first choice. Always be ready to reinforce the right behavior and prevent the wrong one from happening as best you can. Have a leash hanging by the door so that you are ready to prevent jumping on guests, and have a container of treats ready to reinforce sitting.

For the new behavior to replace the old well-established behavior, it must be heavily reinforced with things the dog finds rewarding. A reward can come in the form of attention, a game, an opportunity, or a treat—anything the dog considers reinforcing.

If you're not prepared to train, don't allow your dog to greet the visitor. If you want to fix behavior that is deep-rooted, you have to combat it with well-timed repetitions, a high rate of rewards, and frequent practice around distractions. It may seem awkward at first to carry your clicker and treats with you all the time, but it is essential to capture the moment your dog makes the right choice.

Overall, learning this way is more like real life for the dog, and the learning tends to become more permanent because the dog begins to realize that her commands work everywhere. The more distractions she gets to practice around, the quicker she will learn to generalize her response to your commands.

Control the Variables

Controlling the variables means controlling what's shifting your dog's attention away from you. Distractions often ruin the best-laid plans simply because they are too stimulating for the dog to ignore. If you control the frequency, type, and distance of the distractions, you will increase the speed with which your dog learns. If ringing the doorbell sends your dog into a frenzy, you may want to work on desensitizing him to the doorbell sound first; then you can move on to actually greeting the visitor. In this example, the dog's response to the doorbell and the dog's response to the person would be considered two separate issues.

Other variables might include things that move (such as balls, off-leash dogs, cars, kids, and runners), environmental factors like being outside, or the presence of food. The key points to keep in mind for getting your dog to be successful around these distractions is controlling the distance between your dog and the distraction, and controlling the intensity of the distraction. For your dog's training program to be successful, you need to find your dog's critical distance, and work from there.

QUESTION?

How does "critical distance" relate to training a dog?
The critical distance is the minimum distance between the dog and the distraction. If she is too close to the distraction, it will be difficult for her to pay attention, and she will be less likely to respond to the command.

The distance at which the dog notices the distraction but will still perform the behavior is the starting point. In subsequent training sessions, decrease that distance until she is able to work while the distractions are close by. You will immediately notice that the distance between your dog and the action is an important factor in the success of your training sessions. If the dog is overstimulated by the distraction, she will not be able to ignore it and will not perform the behaviors you ask of her.

The second point to keep in mind when working around distractions is to pay attention to how much of a distraction you are working with. To decrease the intensity of a distraction, offer less movement, fewer dogs, people, kids, or other visual stimuli before attempting to teach the dog any-thing. As your dog starts to learn to ignore distractions and perform the behavior well, you can gradually increase the intensity until he is working in the middle of the distraction.

ALERT!

Too often we assume because the dog is intelligent, she knows what we want. Dogs are perceptive and smart, but they can't read minds. Take the time to teach your dog what you want her to do and make sure you have taught her to do it reliably and in any environment.

As you train your dog to respond to you regardless of where you are and what is happening, your goal over time is to decrease the distance and increase the intensity of the distractions so that your dog will pay attention to you and respond to you regardless of what else is going on. Doing this in a slow sequence of progressions will help you attain your goals more quickly and reliably.

Prevention Is Half the Cure

Human nature is to notice what is going wrong and point it out. When trying to change behavior in animals, putting pressure upon an animal to change the choices it has made is a waste of time since the animal cannot change the past any more than you can.

If you want to make a difference in a future behavior, you must set up the animal for success. Limit her options, provide good consequences for the correct choices, and prevent or provide negative consequences for the wrong choices. Because the animal has choices, the learning is more per-manent and the consequences will directly shape her response.

Pointing out a mistake acts as reinforcement and can actually teach the person or animal to make that same mistake over and over again. A much better approach to changing behavior permanently is to avoid reinforcing the wrong behavior in the first place. If possible, prevent the behavior from happening entirely. During the teaching phrase, it is important to avoid giving the dog any attention for the wrong behavior and concentrate on noticing what's going right. This also means that you should be ready to reward the unexpected good behavior your dog offers every time it happens. If you're not prepared to click and treat, then shower your pup with lots of praise and pats or games and opportunities.

FACT

Remember that prevention can come in the form of a leash, a crate, or a gate—anything that keeps the dog from practicing the wrong behavior while you teach her an alternate response.

Taking It on the Road

Get your dog to respond to all of her commands in new environments by training her everywhere. This will lead to generalization; the dog will be able to perform the behavior regardless of the distractions. Dogs need your help to get them on track in new environments.

The best way to help a dog whose behavior falls apart in a new environment is to go back to kindergarten. Help the dog perform the behavior with a treat or toy as a lure. The idea is to drill the dog for five to ten repetitions to get her working again and then wean her off of the extra help. Repeating the command when the dog is obviously too distracted to hear what you are saying is not teaching the dog anything but how to ignore you. With a little patience and practice, it won't be long before your dog understands that her training works everywhere, regardless of the distraction.

Solutions to Breed-Specific Behavior Problems

Dogs with persistent behavior problems are often exhibiting behavior that is related to the job they were bred to do—herding, retrieving, guarding, or chasing things that move. When a dog has a behavior problem related to its original working ability, think of it as hard-wired behavior or a behavior that a dog's genetics have preprogrammed him to do. Consider the Border Collie that chases and nips at heels, the retriever that is obsessed with having everything in her mouth, or the terrier that barks or chases squirrels. In these cases, the genetics of the dog determines his behavior.

ALERT!

When teaching your dog to generalize her behavior, a good rule of thumb is to give only one command. If the dog doesn't respond appropriately, get out a treat and help the dog perform the behavior. Repeated commands will condition your dog to respond more slowly to commands in public places.

Constant and Patient Reinforcement

What hard-wiring means for you is that without the appropriate training and practice, it will be harder to stop the dog from practicing the undesirable behavior. Here are several things to keep in mind when you are retraining dogs like this:

- Keep the rate of reinforcement high.
- Build up your dog's bank account for good behavior.
- Train your dog to perform the behavior for a longer period of time.
- Consider teaching a trick as a replacement behavior.

If you are going to change the dog's mind about an instinctive behavior, you need to provide lots of reinforcement for the alternate behavior. A high rate of reinforcement means that you keep your standards low and reward the dog for even attempting the new behavior. You don't up your criteria or expect multiple repetitions; you simply reward the new behavior as often as possible. This way it will be more likely for your dog to respond to a given situation with the right behavior because he has been rewarded so frequently.

Money in the Bank

Each reward for the new behavior is money in the bank. You are building a reinforcement history that has to compete with a natural and self-rewarding behavior. Building a strong reinforcement history takes time and practice before it will eventually replace the old hard-wired behavior with the new desirable one.

FACT

Money in the bank is each click and treat for the right behavior. No one can ever have too much positive reinforcement for good behavior. When you are trying to change hard-wired behavior, you must increase the likelihood that your dog will offer the right behavior by making sure the bank account is full.

Practice Makes Perfect

The more you work with your dog, the fewer behavior problems you will have. You are spending time building up a history, and if you are successful your dog will associate training with fun. Teaching your dog to perform tricks is a great way to help you get to know your dog and improve your relationship with him; plus, training tricks is fun and most people enjoy spending time training their dogs this way.

Some dogs love learning tricks more than anything else, so they are more willing to work longer and perform with enthusiasm. If you prefer to teach your dog tricks, why not use them in everyday life to help prevent your dog from practicing inappropriate behaviors? If your dog is a puller, mix in Roll Over, Sit Up Pretty, or Spin with reinforcing the dog for staying with you. To use tricks to replace problem behavior, the dog must know the trick very well in all different kinds of environments, and she also has to be heavily reinforced (at least initially) for choosing to perform the trick rather than the inappropriate behavior. The more you practice what you want, the better it will happen for you when you truly need it. The more creative you are in your training program, the better your relationship with your dog will be.

The most important key to successfully training a more desirable behavior is to have patience. Not all dogs learn at the same rate. Each dog is an individual and is motivated by different things. Be flexible in what type of reward you offer your dog. Be ready to break things down into smaller steps, and be generous with your reinforcement and feedback.

The Bark Stops Here!

Barking can be a hot issue in any neighborhood (see Chapter 12). The dog's reasons for barking will determine what solution will work for your dog. Try to identify whether the dog is bored, unsocialized, fearful, or just too exuberant. Then try different approaches to see what works best for you and your dog. Here are some options to consider:

- Hide treat-stuffed Kong toys all over the yard to prevent boredom.
- Teach your dog to retrieve a toy and carry it to the visitor to help keep your dog quiet.
- Teaching your dog to Roll Over will use up some of the energy that was previously focused on barking.
- Teaching your dog to Spin will keep her too busy to bark.
- Asking for a play Bow is a nice greeting for an elderly person or small child.
- For a dog that likes to use her paws, teaching her to Wave will direct her energy appropriately.

Training your dog to use an alternate behavior will revolutionize the way other people see your dog. It will make your guests comfortable, keep you calm, and give everyone reason to reinforce your dog's good behavior with lots of love and attention.

The best way to get rid of a barking problem is to recognize when the dog is about to erupt and interrupt and redirect his behavior toward a more appropriate venue. This takes practice, and you'll have to know your dog well to time your intervention. You'll also have to know behavior or activity will entertain your dog sufficiently to keep her from barking.

Mugging Company at the Door

Jumping is a problem most dogs do not outgrow. Dogs mainly jump in their exuberance to greet a person and to welcome them to play. Teaching your dog an alternate greeting behavior may be an excellent solution for your dog's jumping problems. Here's how:

- Require a Sit/Stay or Down/Stay before people are allowed to pet your dog.
- Ask your dog to Play Dead or Belly Up and let the visitor scratch her belly as a reward.
- Teaching your dog to Roll Over and Spin, one right after the other, is an excellent way to keep even the most energetic dog focused on her job of greeting sanely.
- Have your dog go fetch a toy to keep her mouth busy and his feet off the company.
- A Stay command can keep her away from the open door and the big wide world beyond.

Though there is no quick solution to jumping, preventing it from happening in the first place is a good start toward changing your dog's first response to visitors. Remember that dogs do what works. If something is no longer an option, it gets eliminated from the list of possibilities and is eventually replaced by what does work. Make sure the behavior that works for your dog is something that works for you, too!

Who's Walking Whom

Pulling on the leash is by far the number one complaint from dog owners and the most common reason they bring their dogs to obedience class. Adding tricks to your dog's repertoire will help you manage her on-leash behavior and give you more options when she starts pulling. If she never knows what you might ask her to do next, she'll be more likely to pay attention to you and less likely to pull.

Teaching your dog appropriate leash manners can be time consuming and tedious; break it up a little with some of these ideas:

- Play the targeting game as you walk by having your dog touch your hand or pant leg with her nose as you walk along.
- As you are walking, stop every so often and ask your dog to Spin.
- Don't walk a long distance all at once without changing direction or frequently stopping to have your dog Sit.
- Mix up moving by asking your dog to stop and Wave.
- Stop periodically and ask your dog to Roll Over several times in a row; it will take the edge off an excitable dog.

Using tricks while teaching your dog to remain under control on leash is an excellent way for her to learn to control her enthusiasm. Directing her energy toward more a appropriate behavior will teach her to pay attention to you and what you are asking her to do. Remember that your dog has been pulling you along behind her for a long time. Since there is a lot of money in your dog's bank account for pulling, you'll need to counter that with huge jackpot deposits for not pulling. This requires frequent practice and a commitment to make sure you don't follow your dog when she is pulling you.

Fierce or Fearful

Aggression and fearfulness are two behavior problems that are stressful for both the dog and the handler. Keeping your dog from getting too overwhelmed and redirecting her attention to you is your primary goal as the owner of a fearful or aggressive dog. Keep in mind that your ultimate goal is to help your dog establish a positive association with the things she is afraid of through positive reinforcement. What better way to do that than to teach her to do tricks in situations where she normally reacts with aggression or fear?

- Teach her to look at you for an extended period of time on command.
- Teach her to touch your hand with her nose.
- Teach her to touch an object or a person's hand. (This has to be built up to slowly.)
- Teach her to Spin or turn around.
- Teach her to Bow; this may help lighten up dogs that are passing by and help your dog feel more relaxed with their presence.
- Teach her to Wave.
- Teach her to Roll Over, which will disorient her enough that she won't know where the scary person or dog disappeared to by the time she's finished.
- Teach her to Say You're Sorry, which will flatten her into a very submissive position—a great way to diffuse other dogs.

The purpose of teaching a fearful or aggressive dog tricks is that when a dog is performing tricks—and trained to ignore distractions—she is concentrating on something else. Think of this as another form of "incompatible behavior."

Knowing exactly what your dog needs for reinforcement is a better, more permanent way to get rid of behavior problems. Noticing what is going right and rewarding it will make it more likely that your dog will replace her old habits with more appropriate good dog manners. Remember what you pay attention to is what you get; if you start ignoring what is going wrong and start rewarding what is going right, the behaviors you see as problems now will disappear and you will be rewarded with a more well-behaved companion.

When Things Go Wrong

When you have made a training plan and it isn't going quite the way you think it should, it is often because you have made the steps too difficult for the dog to accomplish. Breaking behaviors down into small steps is the key to the success of any training program. The easier it is for the dog to be right—especially in the beginning—the more successful your program will be. It is a good idea for the trainer to have the plan written out so that adjustments can be made and steps can be added or broken down into smaller increments if it doesn't go as planned. Don't ever be afraid to go back and make things easier for the dog. Confidence comes from feeling successful. You will quickly make progress when a dog feels confident.

Flexibility

Being flexible in your training plan means being able to see when a dog is struggling and going back and making it easier to be right. It also means that when a dog is successful you know how to increase the difficultly just enough to challenge the dog and push the behavior along without making it so difficult that he quits. If there's one mistake new trainers make, it's being too rigid in what they reinforce. The best way to experience success is to be a splitter rather than a lumper. A lumper looks for big chunks of behavior to reinforce; a splitter shapes the behavior in tiny steps.

Two Approaches to Teaching Down

A good example of this is in teaching the down behavior. Most lumpers just wait for the dog to lie down and will often use a food lure or a gentle shove if that isn't producing the right results. A splitter takes the behavior apart and reinforces smaller versions of the behavior on the way to the end goal of lying down. A splitter might reinforce standing still, then sitting, then sitting with the head down, then lowering the head, then leaving the head low, then bending the elbows, then moving onto a hip until the dog lays all the way down. It can be a lot of work, but the payoff is a dog that understands what you want, can give it to you on cue, and can quickly be retrained around any distraction.

Classical Conditioning Tools

Classical conditioning is the pairing of a scary object or event with something the dog perceives as pleasant, such as a yummy treat or a toy or game. The pairing of two things addresses the problem on an emotional level and is called pretraining. Classical conditioning can be used to address fear and phobia issues and avoidance problems like not liking to have nails trimmed or being reluctant to get into the car or the bathtub. Most frightened dogs will stop eating and playing, which is a great indication that they are also too uncomfortable to learn. Calming them by working on pairing good things with scary things will help them work through their fears and be able to function more happily in daily life. There is a specific way to do this pairing for the dog to associate the scary object, person, or situation with the good thing. Here are some basic guidelines to follow:

- The sessions must be short and not rehearsed; this is pairing, not training.
- The food should remain hidden until after the dog notices the scary object.
- The dog should be at a comfortable distance from the feared object and should not be panicky.
- Appetite is a good indication of comfortable distance. If the dog can eat a treat, you're good. If not, back up.
- Don't try more than two or three repetitions per training session, or the dog will not learn that the scary object makes the good stuff appear.
- The more random the sessions are, the better the dog will predict that good things happen when the scary object is present.

This tool is widely used in helping dogs to become more comfortable in their own skin, and both dog and family benefit from this.

Barking Problems and Solutions

Dogs bark to communicate with us and with each other, but excessive barking is inappropriate and a symptom of a larger problem. If a dog barks excessively, it means that the dog's mental, emotional, and physical needs are not being met. This problem must be addressed first, before peace and quiet reign.

Why Do Dogs Bark Excessively?

A barking dog is a common problem among dog owners and is often the top complaint of neighbors who listen to the restless protests of a dog confined to a yard and bored to death. Dogs are pack animals with strong bonds to their family members; it is unnatural for them to be alone for hours at a time. In their boredom and frustration, they tend to bark, which is self-reinforcing. Barking is an emotional release, a way for a dog to express its emotion and let out bottled-up anxiety and frustration.

A dog that barks too much falls into one of three categories: the dog that barks when left alone; the dog that barks at visitors, noise, and people passing by while you are home; and lastly the dog that barks at you for attention. Excessive barking is a symptom of a larger issue. In general it means that the dog needs something that he isn't getting or is being consistently reinforced for the wrong behavior.

Thinking creatively about changing your dog's environment may give you a little more peace and quiet. Consider planting a row of bushes in your yard, or close the front blinds to block your dog's view of the neighborhood. Distractions will be less apparent to her, and she won't feel the need to bark as much.

Meet Your Dog's Needs

All dogs need a healthy diet, a predictable schedule, lots of exercise, interaction with people and other dogs, training, a safe place to sleep and rest, and a stimulating environment with toys and things to chew. Dogs also need to be taught from the time they are puppies to be content when they are away from you so that they come to expect that you will return predictably to take care of their needs.

Finding a Happy Medium

Just like people, well-adjusted dogs are happy. Finding a healthy balance between time alone and time with people is essential for the emotional well-being of any dog. Dogs that are with their owners all the time can also become excessive barkers when their owners do leave them even briefly. These dogs become inappropriately bonded to their owners and in their absence find it difficult to cope with being alone. This overattachment between owner and dog can erode the dog's self-confidence and contentment when they are alone. Take a moment to examine how much or how little time you spend with your dog and make the necessary adjustments to help him feel confident and secure.

Mindful Management

The next few sections review some basic elements of what you need to keep in mind while you come up with a plan to curb (or at least cut down) your dog's barking. The philosophy is the same for training any behavior: Have a plan, be patient, be consistent, and reinforce the right behaviors.

Doin' What Comes Naturally

Some breeds are prone to barking, but all dogs can learn not to bark excessively or inappropriately. If you have a breed that is known for barking, nip the problem in the bud while the dog is still a pup. Some dogs were bred for their ability to chase or guard, and barking is sometimes part of the package.

If you know what sets your dog off into a frenzy of barking, think carefully about how you can prevent these episodes from happening. The more barking your dog does, the more she gets reinforced for barking. The more reinforcement a behavior gets, the more likely the behavior is to occur and become stronger. If you want to have a quieter household, you need to find your dog's triggers for barking and short circuit as many of them as you can.

Set a Reasonable Goal

A dog that barks a lot isn't going to just quit one day when you find the magic cure. Barking is reinforcing to dogs, and it often gets worse before it gets better. Sit down with your family and set a reasonable goal for your dog. Maybe your dog is the type that barks when the doorbell rings; in this case, your goal might be that she's allowed to bark for thirty seconds and then she must be quiet when you tell her to be quiet. Or if she hears a noise, she can let you know something's going on but then must stop barking and go to her bed. It really doesn't matter what the goal is, so long as it is simple and fairly easy for the dog to do.

It is your job to sit down, agree on something reasonable, and teach it to the dog. Don't be afraid to set small goals and build up the time the dog is required to be quiet by seconds. It isn't reasonable to expect a dog that has been barking excessively for years to suddenly quit overnight.

FACT

To change your dog's response to a typical antecedent to barking like the doorbell, ring the doorbell at random times and give the dog a handful of delicious treats or play a favorite game like tug or fetch. Your ignoring both the bell and the door will teach your dog an alternate expectation to the ringing of the doorbell.

Find the Antecedents to Barking

An antecedent is the trigger or the cause of a behavior. For instance, your dog barks at the sound of a knock or a doorbell. The knock or doorbell would be considered the antecedent for the behavior of barking. Knowing what triggers your dog's barking can be crucial to teaching her to be quiet. The pattern or chain of reaction goes like this: antecedent, behavior, consequence, appropriate behavior, reward. You need to complete this entire circuit of behavior to teach your dog not to bark excessively.

A good way to find antecedents is to keep a chart of when your dog barks and what happens right before she barks. Write down exactly what you think triggered the barking and time how long it took her to stop. If you time how long it takes your dog to calm down, you will know when you are making progress in your training program and when you are spinning your wheels. You'll know you're on track if the number of seconds it takes your dog to calm down becomes smaller over time. Good dog trainers chart progress to see results!

Set the Consequences

For dogs that keep at it and barely take a breath between barks, you may want to use something to interrupt the barking. This way you will be stopping the barking for a second so that you can reward him for being quiet. A consequence is the same as punishment, so alone it will only stop the behavior. It will not teach the dog what he should do instead.

Some ideas for consequences might be a squirt of water, a loud noise, shaking a can of pennies, a nonelectric no-bark collar. (This device is worn around the neck and distracts the dog by squirting a blast of citronella when she barks.) Consequences are used to interrupt the behavior of excessive barking to get the dog to stop for a second so he could be rewarded for being quiet. You will want to plan out ahead of time what the dog should do instead of barking so that you know what behavior to reinforce.

ALERT!

If you only correct the dog for barking and fail to reward him for being quiet, you will get a dog that eventually goes back to barking because he isn't being reinforced for anything else. Remember, what gets rewarded gets repeated.

Notice the Right Stuff

Too often with a noisy dog, we tend to notice only when she is barking and not when she is quiet. A good part of the solution for barking is catching and reinforcing the dog for being quiet. Each reinforcement you provide for a quiet behavior will be money in the bank for a quieter dog overall. Pay attention to your dog at times like this by petting or playing with her, giving her a treat, bringing her inside, letting her outside, opening the crate door, and so on. Whatever would be reinforcing at the moment, reward your dog with it, and you will notice that your dog barks less over the course of several days or weeks, depending on the value of the reinforcement and the severity of the problem.

Remember that barking is just like any bad habit; it is easier to slip back into old patterns of behavior because they are familiar and sometimes reinforcing. Management and prevention is critical.

Set for Success

If you live in a busy neighborhood, be smart. Letting your dog have unsupervised free access to your yard is not a good idea. She will only find things to bark at, effectively reinforcing her obnoxious behavior over and over. This poor management encourages more barking, because dogs think that barking is fun and will continue the behavior in the absence of anything better to occupy their time. Setting up your dog to succeed means that you use prevention to help your dog to be quiet, and then make sure you notice and reward her for *being* quiet. The following are some tips for setting your dog up to succeed:

- **Give her exercise.** A dog can never have too much. Try play dates with other dogs, games of fetch, Frisbee, hide-and-seek, doggie day care, pet sitters, dog walkers, or anyone who will exercise your dog for you.
- **Occupy her.** Try interesting toys, bones, and chew treats that let your dog exercise his jaws. Dogs that bark are often big chewers, so make sure your dog has plenty of good stuff to chew.
- **Pay attention to her.** Be there to supervise and redirect your dog. When you are present in the yard, for instance, practice calling your

dog away from what she is barking at and reward her for engaging in a different behavior.

- **Keep her busy.** Stuff hollow toys with peanut butter and dry dog food, and hide them all over the house and yard; this will give her something to do while you are out.

- **Remove the antecedent.** Prevent barking as often as possible by blocking her view with shrubs, closing the blinds, or rearranging the furniture. Not allowing your dog to practice the wrong behavior is more than half the cure.

- **Meet her needs.** Have a schedule and stick to it as much as possible. Hire a professional dog walker or a doggie day care to help you with walks and exercise if necessary. The more predictable your dog's routine, the better it is for her. Try to feed, walk, and play with your dog on a predictable schedule so that she will learn to trust you and feel secure.

- **Be ready.** It is very important to be ready to reinforce what's going right. Make a plan with your family and stick to it. The more you know what you want, the more likely you are to get it.

- **Use a marker signal.** The use of a clicker to identify which behavior is rewardable (the quiet behavior) is crucial information for the dog, and it is difficult to provide it any other way. Remember that the click marks the quiet behavior so you can then follow through with the reward.

Find the methods that work best for your dog and be patient and consistent in marking her desirable behavior.

Motivation Determines Solutions

Since consequences drive behavior, is it worthwhile to take a few moments over the course of a week or so and observe your dog and what circumstances cause him to bark. Recording what causes the barking to start and how long it takes for him to stop is useful if you want to curb a problem barker. Knowing that it normally takes your dog ten minutes to stop barking after the doorbell rings gives a baseline for barking. While we are implementing a training program to stop the barking, we want to know if the dog is barking for less time as we progress with the training. If the amount of time it takes the dog to stop barking is not getting shorter, it's time to change the plan. Having a baseline helps the trainer break the solution down into small increments and set reasonable goals. A dog that has been barking all its life isn't likely to cease barking forever no matter how much training we do. A more reasonable goal with a dog like this is to have the dog quit barking in a shorter amount of time.

After careful observation, you may find that your dog's barking is caused by just one or two things that happen during the day, like the doorbell ringing and the garbage truck going by. With this information, you can better formulate a training plan to desensitize him to the sound or sight of a barking trigger or train him to do a behavior he couldn't possibly do while barking, such as retrieving a toy or performing a trick. Train him to perform the incompatible behavior when the stimulus (the doorbell or garbage truck) happens.

Barking is usually an emotional thing for dogs. Many dogs bark out of loneliness or frustration, some bark because they want attention or are frightened, and some bark because they like to hear their own voices. Knowing the motivation for barking will help you come up with a creative solution that will make your house a much more quiet and peaceful escape from the world.

Dogs That Bark at Visitors

Dogs that go berserk over visitors may be fearful, overexcited, or downright aggressive to people entering your home. A new pattern of behavior is necessary to teach the dog to respond to visitors in a more appropriate way.

If your dog is aggressive or fearful of strangers, you will probably want to enlist the help of a qualified professional dog trainer or behaviorist to help you evaluate your dog and correctly identify the problem. This person will also help you set up training sessions to help your dog learn better greeting manners and be safe doing it. The biggest task to be tackled is to change your dog's mind about how she feels about company. Here's how:

1. Put the dog out of the room and let your company come in and sit down.
2. After about ten minutes, let your dog out and have everyone ignore her.
3. Arm each person with the yummiest treats and have visitors drop those treats all around their feet.
4. Let your dog be the one to go to the visitor to take the treats.

Congratulations! You just performed your first huge deposit for stopping barking at visitors. Repeat this as often as you can with lots of different people until your dog begins to look forward to having company at the door. You may want to practice this scenario with your own family first to teach the dog this new pattern of behavior and to help the family members learn a new way of managing the dog around company.

To speed up your dog's learning, leave a basket of your dog's favorite toys outside your front door so that visitors are armed with a toy as soon as you open the door. This will distract your dog from barking and help her develop a new habit in greeting guests at the door.

If you're not prepared to train your dog on a given occasion, remove her from the stimuli so at least you're not reinforcing the old pattern of behavior and losing ground. Putting the dog in a separate room or in her crate will at least make sure she doesn't fall back to her old ways.

Friendly Options

Dogs that bark because they are happy to see company simply need distractions to keep them quiet. Teaching your dog to grab a stuffed animal on her way to the door will keep her mouth busy and make it impossible for her to bark and hold the toy at the same time. This is what is meant by teaching your dog to do something that is incompatible with barking. A dog can't bark with a toy in her mouth.

This works best for dogs who love toys. The shaping steps are as follows:

1. Toss or hand a toy to your dog to get her to grab it. Label this Get It.
2. Pair the command with the doorbell. Tell your dog to Get It, toss her a toy, and cue the doorbell. Eventually, the doorbell becomes the cue for picking up a toy.

You'll want to make sure you pick a toy your dog really loves so that she'll want to hold the toy more than she'll want to bark. You can even leave a basket of toys by the door and let your visitor select one to greet your dog with. This will teach your dog that visitors are fun but that barking isn't part of that fun. Take advantage of any willing helpers like neighbors, fellow dog lovers, and friends. The more your dog gets to practice greeting guests quietly, the better for everyone. Take your time and experiment with different toys to see which ones become your dog's favorites and keep her so engrossed that she forgets to bark!

ALERT!

Recreational barkers bark for the sheer joy of it. Owners often find that teaching tricks, or playing a dog sport like agility or Rally obedience keeps these dogs active and engaged enough to minimize their barking. The key to success is training these dogs to control themselves by teaching them that calm behaviors get rewarded.

Taming Doorbell Madness

Dogs that burst into action at the sound of the doorbell will need some help in getting over this huge stimulus before they can be expected to be quiet. The sound of the doorbell ringing may be your dog's antecedent to barking and the most difficult of distractions for her. Most dogs with this problem explode into a cacophony of shrill barking and take several minutes to calm down.

The best way to manage these dogs is to teach them an alternative response to the ringing doorbell. The easiest and noisiest way to do this is through a process called "flooding." Flooding involves ringing the doorbell a billion times when no one is there for the dog to greet so that it eventually doesn't mean what the dog thinks it means. She will start to develop an alternative response to the doorbell and come to expect something different from what she originally thought.

QUESTION?

Is there a trick to getting the dog to stop barking for attention?
It is important that everyone in the family be committed to ignoring the dog when he barks for attention and absolutely not give in to the dog's demands. The more the behavior of barking for attention doesn't work, the faster the problem behavior will disappear.

You can also add a bit of classical conditioning to change the dog's association with the doorbell. Classical conditioning is about developing associations between a noise or object, in this case the doorbell, and something good, like a treat or a game of fetch. To incorporate conditioning into the training, ring the bell and shower the dog with treats or start throwing a ball around regardless of the dog's behavior (barking or not).

Here, we are not requiring the dog to do something before she gets something, as in operant conditioning or clicker training. To the novice trainer, it may seem at first that we are rewarding the dog for barking when we ring the bell and treat the dog. In reality we are trying to form an association between the doorbell and something good so that eventually instead of barking, your dog will be expecting a treat, a game, a toy, or a pat from the visitor. This can be a very powerful tool in trying to change your dog's association with doorbells. Using it to help solve your barking problem may get you where you want to go faster than through other methods.

Dogs That Bark for Attention

Some dogs have their owners all figured out. Remember that most dogs don't work for a living and have nothing else to do but sit around and watch you. They know just what to do to get what they want by barking at you until they get it. When a dog barks at you for attention, it usually means that he is confused about who's in charge in the family and may not have enough rules and limits put upon him to give him a clue as to where he falls in the family hierarchy.

A two-pronged approach almost always works for these needy dogs. First, stop paying attention to them when they are barking. Second, start noticing, marking, and rewarding them for being quiet. Walk away, turn your head to the side, or turn your back on your dog to let him know that what he is doing is not rewardable. If your dog is used to getting his way by barking, this method of management may take a while, but overall it is a faster process and more productive than constantly yelling at the dog to be quiet.

Head Halters

You will find several types of training equipment you can use to shorten your training time and gently help your dog relax and trust that you are in charge. The Gentle Leader Headcollar is one such head halter. Head halters are excellent equipment to own. With the proper introduction, they will cut your training time in half (see Chapter 15).

ALERT!

Introduce the head collar slowly and with lots of goodies and positive associations. The more positively you introduce your dog to this piece of equipment, the more useful it will be to you. If you rush it, your dog's resistance will make the halter a hindrance rather than a help.

The original purpose of the head halter is to teach dogs not to pull on the leash. It does this by guiding them under the chin. In essence, when a dog is wearing one of these, you control his forward movement by controlling his head. The head halter has an added benefit, too: When fitted correctly, it puts gentle pressure on two points on the dog's head and neck, which help relax the dog and makes him feel more secure.

Some dogs find the effect so calming that they forget to bark and are overall more relaxed and mellow. Head halters should be introduced very slowly if they are to be a useful tool for you. Dogs need to be taught to wear head halters, but once they like wearing them, it can have an amazing effect on their behavior.

Canine Massage

An often overlooked method of achieving a quieter dog is canine massage. The massage technique most worthy of mention for changing unwanted behavior is called Tellington TTouch, or TTouch. It was developed for horses by Linda Tellington-Jones, and it has been applied to all kinds of animals for all kinds of behavior problems.

Dogs hold a lot of their emotions in their faces and mouth areas, and most dogs that are tense or hyperactive tend to bark and chew to relieve anxiety. In general, dogs that are restless, overactive, aggressive, or excessive barkers often have a chewing or biting problem as well. These animals can benefit from a bit of therapeutic massage on their muzzles and gum lines.

The best T-touch technique involves making small circles on the muzzle and jaw line with the tips of the fore and middle fingers. You'll want to lightly move the skin in a clockwise direction for a full circle, then pick your hand up and do another circle right next to it. Take your time and make each circle for a count of five. Breathe in and out naturally and relax so that the dog will relax too. Animals know when we hold our breath, and it makes them tense.

You may want to start getting your dog used to this by sitting on a chair or the floor and having your dog sit between your feet. Support under his jaw with one hand while you make circles with the other. Use a light pressure, about as much as would be comfortable if you made a circle on your eyelid. You can even slip your finger under the dog's lip and make small circles on the gum line itself. You may want to wet your fingers first if your dog has a dry mouth.

There's Always Hope for the Problem Barker

Barking can be problematic for owners and neighbors alike, but it doesn't have to be. Owning a pet should be an enjoyable experience, and barking should not get in the way of enjoying your pet, but the time to act is now. The longer you let your dog reward himself by getting what he wants when he barks, the more barking you will have to listen to.

Put together a training plan that will help reform your barking lunatic into the quiet companion you've always wanted. You have the tools to change the behavior. Now it's time to get to work. Take the time to look seriously at the ways in which you are meeting your dog's basic needs for exercise; changing this by increasing your dog's playtime with other dogs is often a huge factor in cutting down on the amount of barking you are listening to. Most of all, don't give up. Even the most obnoxious barker can be taught to be a quieter, more enjoyable companion. He just needs to be trained.

CHAPTER 13

Fears and Phobias

A fearful dog is a challenge to own and train. In familiar surroundings, he is a sweet, wonderful family pet, but in new places where there are strange sounds and people, he turns into a mess of jittery shaking nerves. If you own a dog like this, it is important to educate yourself and learn all you can to help your dog become a less fearful and more confident companion.

Make a Commitment to Training

Fearful dogs do not suddenly become confident, even with lots of training. Training a fearful dog to be more confident is a time-consuming project that is best undertaken with a determined attitude and clear, achievable goals. Being specific about how you want your dog to react and behave is a huge step toward making it a reality.

Be Organized and Consistent

When training a fearful dog, it is important to be flexible. You will not always move in a forward direction. Sometimes it will feel like you move one step forward and ten steps back. Being flexible enough to realize when you've pushed too hard and being insightful enough to know what changes to make so that your dog is successful are two of the most important elements of a successful dog trainer.

ALERT!

Fearful dogs operate on emotion. They do not really think about what they are doing, and therefore no amount of correction or comforting will help them get over it and act like they do at home. If you take on the project of working with a dog like this, you will have to learn to be patient and flexible.

Having a regular schedule of training is important in training any dog, but it is absolutely critical when working with a fearful dog. Breaking your goals down into steps is the key to seeing improvement in a relatively short period of time.

Using Targeting

Targeting can be a useful tool for fearful dogs. For instance, maybe your dog is afraid of strange men. You may start off by using a male member of your family that your dog likes and teach your dog to target the person's hand (see Chapter 4).

Targeting involves the dog approaching the strange person and touching her nose to the person's hand. This, of course, would need to be broken down into really tiny pieces if the dog is really afraid of the strange person. For instance, you may want to have the person sit in a chair and ignore the dog at first. Then, you could have the stranger drop small pieces of treats all around his feet and let your dog take her time about going up and eating them. If your dog is too scared to eat, break it down into something even easier, like having the person lie on the couch or sit a greater distance away. Your dog's appetite is a good indicator to her comfort level. If she is too stressed to eat, you need to make changes to see any progress.

FACT

The amount of time you spend training your dog to target will really pay off when you start to apply it in the situations where the dog is afraid. The behavior of targeting becomes a game to the dog if you practice enough.

You would gradually change the variable so that the dog will eventually go and target the person's hand for a click and treat. Most people who have been successful using targeting to teach their dogs to get over their fears have done an extensive amount of training teaching their dogs to target their own hands and the hands of people the dog likes. Targeting can also be used to teach your dog to learn to be brave around scary objects or to learn to jump into the car or bathtub.

You will find that because targeting has such good associations for your dog, she will be more willing to extend himself and be open to new experiences; it will give her something to do instead of being scared. Taking the time to teach your dog how to target will be one of the most important training tools you have to help your dog get over her fears.

Genetics, Abuse, or a Lack of Exposure?

People often assume that fearful dogs have been mistreated by a prior owner or some other person who has had contact with the dog. More commonly, however, dogs are fearful or phobic because they lack early experience with lots of different types of people, sounds, and experiences, including other dogs. Genetics can also play a fairly large role in shaping a dog's fearful behavior, and shyness is a common, though undesirable, trait in some breeds.

It is very important to research who you are buying your puppy from and steer clear of puppy mills, pet stores, and places where more than one breed are bred. Select a responsible breeder. The American Kennel Club (*www.akc.org*) has a breeder referral service on its website.

Breeding

Good breeders are committed to turning out puppies that are healthy, well adjusted, and ready for life. They screen their potential puppy buyers and make sure they educate each buyer so that they train and socialize their puppies appropriately. The reality is you get what you pay for, and quality puppies from good breeders don't come cheap. A lot of love and care goes into each puppy if the breeder does his job right.

If you feel your dog's problems stem from a genetic component, it is still possible to train him. Even in well-bred dogs with conscientious breeders, some puppies can be more fearful than their littermates. If the shyness is identified early enough, intensive socialization and training can yield positive results in a relatively short period of time. The earlier a problem is identified, the better the prognosis. Certain breeds can be more prone to fearfulness, but any dog can grow up being fearful and suspicious of new people and experiences.

A genetic predisposition to noise sensitivity is common in many breeds used for hunting and sporting purposes. Dog breeders who truly care will breed out these traits by choosing only the friendliest, most confident dogs for their breeding programs. If you are looking for a puppy of a breed that has fearful tendencies, ask lots of questions about the parents' temperaments, meet both parents before purchasing the pup, and choose a breeder who has someone perform the puppy aptitude test on all of his litters. Dogs that are carefully bred by knowledgeable, caring people should be friendly and outgoing regardless of their breed.

FACT

The puppy aptitude test is a series of tests performed on forty-nine-day-old puppies that helps determine their tendencies to be outgoing, shy, mischievous, or pushy. You can obtain more information on puppy aptitude testing from DogWise, a dog and cat book retailer, which can be found online at *www.dogwise.com*.

Social Development

If your dog is under a year old and you feel his fearfulness is a result of a lack of early socialization, get out there and get busy. The earlier you start to change this, the more successful your training program will be. The longer you wait, the harder it will be to change.

Consider enrolling your dog in a well-organized group training class. Be honest with your instructor about what your goals are, and ask if a group class would be an appropriate place to start with your dog. Doggie day care facilities often take on special cases, and the staff is knowledgeable about these problems. They can help make sure your dog has an enjoyable day. Don't be afraid to ask questions, and be flexible and consistent with your end of the commitment.

Getting a puppy from a person who has been raising dogs for many years and knows how to provide the right kind of environment will save you time in the long run. If a puppy misses out on these critical early social periods and is not raised in an environment that stimulates him to explore and learn about his world, he will be a fearful, phobic adult dog. Shyness, fears, and fear-related aggression are most likely the result of a lack of socialization than past abuse or mistreatment. Abuse is often used as the excuse for dogs who are fearful or aggressive when in reality a lack of early socialization is at the root of the problem. However, there are mistreated dogs who are fearful and skittish as a result of their experiences. They have learned that strange people and places are scary and dangerous. If your dog has been mistreated, sit down and develop a plan and then get out there and train your dog!

Unrealistic Expectations

The key to success for fearful dogs is to set realistic expectations for their progress. If you weren't expecting your dog to be fearful, you might want to make the fears go away and get on to the good stuff. This isn't an ideal attitude to have if you want to bring about the most change. Dogs that are fearful very rarely just get over their fears, because their fears are caused by a variety of factors that we can't always control. Remember that genetics and early socialization play a huge role in fears and phobias. Not having enough exposure at a young age makes for fearful dogs that don't recover well from frightening events nor have the skills to deal with new situations that cause them stress.

What are some reasonable expectations for a fearful dog? It depends on the dog and what is causing the fear, but in general you are looking for bounce back—the term used to describe how long it takes the dog to recover from a fright. For instance, you are walking your dog and a big truck passes you. Your dog tries to bolt, tucks her tail, and starts panting. Her eyes are dilated, her ears are pinned back, and she's terrified. How long does it take her to recover? A minute, 10 minutes, an hour, never? Knowing how long it normally takes your dog to recover from a fright will help you determine if you are making progress in your training plan or if you are just spinning your wheels. If you are making progress, it is likely that your expectations are reasonable and your training program is right on target. If you are not making progress, you will want to re-evaluate your training program and set lower goals, break things down into smaller pieces, and offer more support to your dog.

Now Get Busy Training

All dogs need structure, but fearful dogs need even more. The more predictable the schedule and house rules, the better able they will be to cope with life. Spoiling or indulging these dogs will make them worse, because above all else, a fearful dog needs a strong, fair, and consistent leader. Providing structure for a fearful dog means feeding, walking, and exercising him at specific times. It means having house rules that are hardly ever broken, such as no dogs on the bed, dog must sit before going outside, eating his meals, or having his leash put on.

No matter what your house rules are, the most important thing is that you have them. A dog that knows what is expected of him will know that someone else is going to take care of him. This alone will give him more confidence. House rules can be flexible, but not until your dog is more confident. The more strict and consistent the rules are, the quicker the dog will be to trust that you can take care of him and the more he will look to you for leadership.

Establish Rules

You can do several things to help raise your dog's confidence level and make it more likely that your training program will be successful.

- **Avoid reinforcing fearful behavior.** Petting and talking soothingly to the dog or picking him up rewards the dog for the fearful behavior. A hands-off approach where you signal that everything is fine will send the message to your dog that there is nothing to fear.
- **No punishment—ever!** There is never a reason for punishment in a situation where a dog is fearful. If a dog is frightened, he is in an emotional state, not a learning state. Physical or verbal correction will only convince him that there really is something to fear. Punishment may even bring out aggression if your dog feels threatened and vulnerable. Avoid any type of correction; it won't get you where you want to go.
- **Safety first.** Keep the leash on at all times in public and make all the exits in your house escape-proof. Deny your dog access to the front door, for instance, if he is constantly looking to dash out the door or tends to panic during thunderstorms or when he hears loud noises.
- **Exercise and mental stimulation.** Dogs that lack confidence need exercise more than ever. Chasing a ball, playing hide-and-seek,

learning tricks, and participating in agility training, fly ball, or any of the various dog sports are all excellent ways for your dog to release his energy reserves and the tensions of the day.

Paying attention to providing the right environment for your dog and making sure that it is one in which he can learn to trust will put you on the road to helping your dog become a more confident and enjoyable companion.

Confidence Training

Fearful dogs don't have to stay that way forever. With lots of patience and careful training, you can help your dog enjoy life just a little more. Keep in mind, however, that building confidence in a fearful dog is time consuming; don't expect miracles overnight. Be flexible in your plans. Be sure to make room for regression, and have a plan as to how you will handle it. Being prepared for setbacks will also help your dog gain confidence more quickly, since his handler will simply shift plans and continue on rather than panic, flounder, and confuse him.

Teaching your dog to target and making a game out of it is a great way to build his confidence. If you practice enough, it becomes second nature to the dog, and he will learn to play it regardless of what else is going on around him. Teaching your dog to target your hand (see Chapter 4) involves your dog bumping your hand with his nose for a click and treat. This can be a powerful tool in building your dog's confidence. Making targeting a game will give you a tool to raise his confidence level regardless of the circumstances, but you must practice a lot for it to be useful.

Going slowly and building your dog's confidence gradually will be money in the bank for less fearful behavior. If you blow it and move too fast, go backward and move more slowly or quit the session and try again another time.

Review the chapter on targeting, and once you've got your dog easily following your hand, transfer the target to another person. Find a helper that the dog knows and have her offer her hand as a target for your dog to touch. You may have to go back to the early steps and have the helper start off with a treat in her hand at first. Gradually increase the distance so that your dog will go across the room to touch the person's outstretched hand. Verbally label the behavior Go Say Hello. Congratulations! You now have a new game to play with your dog and a way to increase his confidence around new people. Practice at every opportunity and be sure to have a backup plan in case he is too fearful to go and target. Having a plan will make it so that you will transition smoothly, and your dog will barely notice that you've changed plans.

Classical Conditioning

Using classical conditioning in your training program can help you cover more ground more quickly because it deals more with associations and feelings than actually requiring the dog to perform a certain behavior. Classical conditioning involves forming an association of "scary thing" equals "good stuff." Good stuff can come in the form of games, toys, food, affection, or anything the dog finds reinforcing. Using this technique can be helpful for dogs that are just too scared to work at all or for noise sensitivities and phobias.

FACT

The most important thing to keep in mind with this type of training is that the dog gets good things regardless of his behavior. Remember that you are trying to form an association between the scary person, noise, or thing and things the dog likes.

The way that classical conditioning works is that each time the noise is present, the bar is open. Throw treats on the ground, play ball, or play a favorite game. When the noise goes away, so does all the good stuff and your attention as well. (Ignore your dog for at least five minutes.) Your goal is to change the dog's association with the feared noise to one of expecting good things to happen.

Using classical conditioning to change your scared dog's behavior is like making huge bank deposits in your dog's bank account. It will complement your dog's operant training program because you have a more relaxed dog to train. Half of the problem of training a scared dog is that he is not relaxed enough to absorb the lesson and therefore requires more repetition and more changes of variables.

Systematic Desensitization

This technique involves playing the noise at a very low volume or keeping the scary person or thing at enough distance so that the dog notices it but does not react fearfully to it. A good rule of thumb is that if the dog won't take a treat or play with you, the volume is too high or the distance is too close. Increase the volume gradually, or bring the person or thing closer, so that eventually the dog will ignore it all together and continue to take treats and play.

FACT

Remember that fearful dogs didn't get that way overnight. A high rate of reinforcement (frequent clicks and treats for anything that is going right) will help you build your dog's bank account for acting confident, and this will help your dog get used to new people or things.

The process of systematic desensitization involves interacting with the dog in a positive way, be it with a game of fetch or teaching tricks, so as to help the dog develop a more positive association with the feared noise or object. The dog starts to associate the feeling of being relaxed around the scary noise or object, and eventually you can increase the volume and decrease the distance until the dog will accept the new thing as part of his environment and no longer finds it threatening.

Teaching tricks would be a great way for the dog to associate fun with noise. If you move slowly enough, you will find that having fun learning and performing tricks is incompatible with acting fearful. With enough patience and practice, you will have a dog that is able to get over his fears because he has learned to trust that only good things happen.

Veterinary Behaviorist and Alternative Solutions

Veterinary behaviorists are skilled both as veterinarians and as dog behavior experts. You may consider the help of a behaviorist to help diagnose your dog's problem and help you start working toward a solution. The main difference between a veterinary behaviorist and a dog trainer/behaviorist is that the veterinary behaviorist can prescribe medication for dogs with problems that are too intense or severe to change with training alone.

Consider seeking the help of a veterinary behaviorist if you don't seem to be making any progress after six weeks or if your dog seems unnaturally fearful. Some dogs are so afraid of being left alone that they will cause injury to themselves or major destruction to their surroundings in the absence of their owners. Dogs like this may benefit from veterinary-prescribed drugs that will help restore chemical balance and assist them in learning appropriate and alternative behavior. If your dog suffers from a chemical imbalance, no amount of training will change that. Restoring the body to its equilibrium will ensure that your dog will be able to make the most of her training sessions and will make progress faster. In most cases, the goal is to wean the dog off the medication by adhering to a strict behavioral program until the dog learns a new response.

Veterinary behaviorists also have experience with difficult or unusual problems, such as excessive tail chasing, shadow chasing, obsessive behaviors, severe separation anxiety, and aggression. A veterinary behaviorist usually charges a substantial fee, which covers the initial visit. On the first visit, the behaviorist will meet your dog and take a complete history to diagnose your dog's problem and advise you on the treatment.

The behaviorist will most likely design a training program for you to follow and require that you give updates on your dog's progress. In some cases, the behaviorist may even refer you to a local obedience trainer to help coach you as you implement the training program. Not all problems require medication, but in some severe cases pharmacological intervention can save you huge amounts of time in training and make the success of your training program that much more likely.

Natural Remedies

If you have a dog that has complex behavioral problems, it is crucial to keep an open mind about alternative methods of treatment, such as massage, acupuncture, and homeopathic remedies. Not all solutions will seem to fit your problems or be something you may have even considered.

Holistic veterinary practitioners may use alternative solutions for fearful dogs. Homeopathic remedies often work to help your dog restore her natural balance so that her body can heal itself. If you decide to go this route, the veterinarian will take a detailed history of your dog's heath and diet and also her likes, dislikes, and general behavioral issues. Consider seeking out a professional to consult with to see what recommendations she might have for your dog. She may use a combination of herbal remedies, body wraps, massage techniques, and behavioral training to help you achieve your goal of a more confident pet. The more alternatives you seek, the more likely you will be to find a solution that will help improve the speed of your dog's training program.

To find alternative practitioners like acupuncturists, chiropractors, massage therapists, or other types of alternative specialists in your area, try asking other dog owners, looking in the yellow pages, asking at your local health food store, contacting the nearest veterinary school, or doing a search on the Internet.

Alternative Solutions

Fear is an emotion that can get in the way of training; because of this, you may find that training alone is not the entire solution. Consider seeking out alternative methods of treatment to be sure you have covered all the bases. Fears are often the result of an injury or underlying medical problem that goes undetected and can often be successfully identified through chiropractic or acupuncture consultations.

There are also lots of different massage techniques available for dogs, including the Tellington TTouch (see page 165). This type of technique helps dogs to become more confident and aware of their bodies and works well in conjunction with a behavior modification program. Regardless of what you start with, the general rule to keep in mind is to do no harm. The more open-minded you are toward trying something new, the more your dog will benefit. If you have a difficult problem, the best approach is to seek out as much information as possible so that you have lots of tools to help your dog live a more comfortable life and make her a more enjoyable companion.

In general, phobic dogs are a mix of unfortunate experiences and a lack of early socialization appropriate for their temperament. Retraining these dogs to be more confident can be a challenge. Changing behavior that is based in fear isn't easy. It requires a huge commitment of time and energy to help your dog learn to cope with life, but the owners who embark on this adventure find the rewards immeasurable. If you are truly committed to making your dog a more confident and participating member of your family, start training your dog today!

CHAPTER 14

Housebreaking 101

Housebreaking problems are the leading cause of abandonment. Owners get frustrated with their pets and make the decision to give up their animals to shelters across the nation. Nothing erodes the bond of man and dog quicker than a puddle or a pile on the carpet. Dogs have a natural housebreaking instinct that involves separating their sleeping place from where they eliminate; we take advantage of this instinct when we housebreak them.

Why Things Go Wrong

If the natural instinct to eliminate away from the sleeping area is missing, it usually means that the puppy was mishandled and not given the opportunity to eliminate outside of the sleeping area. In some cases, the puppy was not raised by a superclean mom that kept the whelping box free of stool. In other cases, the puppy may have spent too much time in a cage in a pet store or a shelter and learned to go in her crate because there was no other option. A puppy that doesn't have this instinct can be a lot more difficult to housebreak. This doesn't mean he can't learn to go in the appropriate place, but it will mean the whole process will take a little longer than average and require you to be more vigilant and flexible with your walking schedule.

Another problem with housebreaking occurs when humans confuse setting limits with being mean or allowing too much freedom too soon. When pups have free run of the house, they go to the bathroom whenever they have to go; as a result, they never learn to hold it. Other pups are not supervised well enough when they have freedom and sneak off to "go" somewhere inappropriate when no one is looking. Almost all housebreaking problems are caused by human error, which is good news. It means that all you need to do is educate yourself so that you, too, can have a pooch that knows where to eliminate.

Using a Crate to Help Housebreak Your Dog

The dog's ancestor, the wolf, housebroke himself by sleeping in a cave and eliminating outside that cave. Through the adult's example, the puppies learned to do the same. We mimic this cave concept when we crate train our dogs. Using a crate is like giving your dog his own bedroom, a place for him to relax and rest without getting into trouble. Being confined to a crate requires that he hold his bladder and bowels to avoid an unpleasant consequence—having to sit in his own mess until you come to rescue him.

ALERT!

Crates are not just for housebreaking. They also help keep your puppy safe while you are away and prevent destructive chewing. Though the crate may not be useful to some people as a housebreaking tool, you may find it extremely useful for getting through all of the destructive phases of your dog's development.

Using a crate gives a clear message to a puppy: "Hold it until I let you out." Such a message takes advantage of his natural instincts to sleep in one place and eliminate in another. Using a crate is the nicest thing you can do for your dog, and if it's used properly, it will help speed up housebreaking. Following are some tips for using a crate:

- A young puppy (less than sixteen weeks) should be in the crate more than she is out and should only be free when you are there to supervise her.
- No food or water should be given in the crate while you are gone.
- No towels or padding in the crate at first until your dog has been dry in the crate for at least two weeks straight. Otherwise, she may go on the towel and then kick it to the back.
- A puppy between the ages of seven and twelve weeks will need to be taken to the potty spot every hour at first and then every two to three hours after that.
- Hire a pet sitter to provide regular walks if you are gone for long periods during the day.
- Puppies twelve to eighteen weeks can last a bit longer between walks, but you should increase the time gradually.
- If your pup cries or barks in the crate, try to ignore her until she is quiet before letting her out. Covering the crate completely with a sheet or towel often helps puppies settle down to sleep faster, especially if they bark and whine a lot.
- When introducing the crate, leave the door open and entice your puppy in and out with treats or toys. You can also use the clicker and treats to encourage your puppy to go in and out of the crate.

- Put your puppy in the crate frequently when you are home so that she gets used to being away from you for gradually longer periods at a time.
- Keep your crate around throughout the first and second year of your dog's life. You will find it a godsend if you have workmen doing repairs, company visiting, or if you travel with your dog. If you teach your dog to like her crate, she will always have a safe place to call her own no matter where she goes.

Dogs that can't use a crate for whatever reason should be supervised constantly and not allowed free access to the rest of the house until they have been reliable with their housebreaking for at least six weeks. Freedom after that should be given gradually until you are certain your dog is reliable.

Charting Your Dog's Progress

Teaching a dog to use the outside for his bathroom needs is not rocket science, but it can be frustrating and time consuming. You won't teach your dog to go outside overnight, but there are some tips that will make sure you are moving in that general direction. One really useful tool in housebreaking a dog is a housebreaking chart to keep track of what time he was walked, if he went, and what he did. A simple chart on the fridge will help the whole family keep track of your puppy's progress and make it easier to know when your puppy can have some freedom and when he should be supervised carefully for signs that he has to go out. Most puppies will sniff the floor and walk in circles when they need to go out.

Keeping a chart will track your pup's progress, but it will also help family members know when to supervise closely and when to allow freedom. If the person who is next in charge of walking the pup checks the chart, he will know to take the puppy out more frequently and watch him closely for signs that he needs to go.

Housebreaking Habits

A young pup between seven and twelve weeks should be walked every hour. It is the repetition of being taken to the same spot time and again that gives him the idea of what he needs to do and where to do it. Pick one spot in the yard, keep him on a leash, and only stay out for about one to three minutes. If he goes, label it something like Hurry Up and play with him, or give him a little freedom in the house or yard. If he doesn't go, crate him or keep him with you, and try again in ten or twenty minutes.

If you allow him to roam the yard on his own, chances are he will have so much fun that he will forget to go and end up coming inside and having an accident on the floor. As your puppy gets to be between twelve and eighteen weeks old, you'll find that he can go longer between potty trips. Use your chart to decide how long that should be.

You can also use your chart to keep track of when your puppy has accidents so that you will know when you need to add in an extra walk or supervise more carefully. Over several weeks of charting, you will be able to put the charts together and determine if you are making progress in the right direction. If you aren't, you'll be able to decide what you need to do to get back on track.

No Papers, Please

Using newspapers or potty pads to housetrain your puppy is the surest way to make him unreliable with housebreaking. Dogs that are trained to "go" on newspaper or potty pads never learn to hold it because they go whenever they have to. If you want to housebreak your dog reliably, don't use paper to train him. Take him outside from day one and don't look back. If you are currently using newspaper, pick it up and throw it away: Start taking your dog outside today.

Some people who have dogs that will weigh less than five pounds as adults choose to teach their dogs to go in a litter box rather than taking them outside. This may be a desirable option for you if you live in a high-rise apartment and it is a long trip to the great outdoors. Using a litter box works on the same principles of paper training except that the actual potty spot is unique and in no way resembles a carpet or any other surface you are likely to have in your house. It would be ideal to keep this litter box on a balcony or sun porch and walk your dog as though he were going outside to do his business. If you leave the litter box indoors and allow your dog free access to it, you will have the same problems you would with a paper-trained dog. If your dog can go whenever he wants, he will never learn to hold it and will likely never be truly housebroken.

ALERT!

Using paper in the house gives your dog the impression that there is a safe place to go inside. When the paper is gone, you will have to walk him more frequently and supervise him more carefully, but he will get the idea over time that the only place he can go is outside.

Using a Leash for Potty Trips

Unless your dog is a rescue dog adopted from a shelter as an adult and absolutely will not go on a leash, it is a good idea to use a leash to take your dog to the potty spot. The leash should be about six feet long. You should stand in one spot; don't follow the dog all over the yard. Let the dog sniff in a circle around you and praise the heck out of her if she goes. Try not to get her into the habit of walking the neighborhood unless you want to do that in freezing cold weather or pouring rain.

The trick to walking your dog on a leash is to get her to go to the bathroom quickly without too much distraction so that your dog will perform her potty duties quickly and on demand regardless of the weather. The leash acts as a way for you to communicate to your dog that you are not outside to play but to take care of the business at hand.

Label It

Dogs that are taught to go to the bathroom on cue are a pleasure to walk. Even in bad weather, they go out and do their business, and their owners don't freeze to death waiting for them. Putting the act of eliminating on a cue by calling it something will help speed up the whole ordeal. The common labels for potty behavior are Go, Hurry Up, or Get Busy.

Through training, you can have each function labeled and your dog will go on command whenever you ask. This is really convenient if you're about to take her inside a store, a friend's house, or the hospital you're visiting as a therapy dog team. Since you know your dog has gone and will last until you leave, you can relax and enjoy your visit. To label the potty behavior, say whatever your command is going to be as your dog is in the process of going. You can even click and treat as she is going to give her the idea that doing her business outside is a good thing. It takes a lot of repetitions for the dog to understand that the command means to "go," so be patient and make sure everyone in the family knows what commands are being used.

ALERT!

A good rule of thumb for potty trips for unhousebroken dogs is to stay out for one to two minutes, tops. If she goes, praise and give her freedom. If she doesn't go, either confine her to a crate or gated area or keep her with you for twenty minutes or so and try again later. The message to the dog is "if you go, you get freedom; if you don't, you don't."

Make a Potty Spot in Your Yard

You may also want to consider creating a potty spot in your yard, a designated place where your dog can do his business without interfering with the beauty of the rest of your yard. Creating one area that clearly says "bathroom" to your dog will help you housebreak her, and it will also keep her from using the whole yard as her toilet. That way if you'd like to have barbecues or let your children play in the yard, you won't have to worry about scooping the whole yard.

To build the potty spot, you'll want to use materials that offer good drainage and the ability to disinfect. Here are some potty spot recommendations:

- Make a square or rectangular box out of garden timbers cut to the dimensions you wish. Large dogs probably need an 8' × 8' area, whereas smaller dogs could probably live with a 4' × 4' space.
- Cover the bottom with several bags of sand.
- Cover the sand with a variety of sizes of crushed stone. Some people prefer the tiny size often called "pea stone;" others prefer the 1-inch diameter.

Designated potty spots will allow you to scoop easily and disinfect with a bleach solution regularly. A weed sprayer with a 30:70 solution of bleach and water works well as a disinfectant. Even in tight quarters, this arrangement eliminates excessive odors and unsanitary conditions. A metal rake may also help you to redistribute the stone and sand.

Confinement Works

Young puppies or even adult dogs that are not housebroken should not have free access to the house. If you allow too much freedom too soon, you will create housebreaking problems. Dogs often consider where they eat and sleep their home. The rest of the house is the outside. That is why a puppy kept in the kitchen will often run to the dining room to piddle or poop if he gets loose. Using a crate to keep your puppy confined when you cannot watch him is an excellent housebreaking tool.

The confinement area should be relatively small to keep the puppy from designating one end for sleeping and the other for the bathroom. This is why a crate works perfectly. It should be large enough for your puppy to stand up in without his shoulders touching the ceiling.

Try not to put any cozy blankets, newspaper, or bedding inside the crate until the dog has proven himself by staying dry in the crate for two weeks straight. For dogs that cannot be crate trained for some reason, confinement by means of baby gates is key. If the dog is walked on a regular basis, he will do his best to keep his gated area clean.

Control the Food and Water

A puppy is like a sieve: What goes in will come out. Pay attention to how much and how often he eats and drinks and regulate what goes in so you can regulate what comes out. Your unhousebroken dog should not have free access to food and water, because he will eat and drink whenever he wants, and you will be less able to predict when he'll need to go out. To housebreak a dog, you need to stick to a strict food and water schedule and be sure that he is walked at regular intervals. Puppies that have a regular feeding routine are easy to predict; if you feed and water them on a schedule, they will go out on schedule.

FACT

Providing a consequence for unproductive trips to the potty spot is a good idea. The most logical consequence is a lack of freedom. A dog that normally goes at a certain hour, like first thing in the morning or last thing at night, should not be allowed to play freely in the house or yard until he has had a productive trip outside.

The best way to help a puppy develop a reliable housebreaking schedule is to feed roughly at the same time each day and not leave water out all day and night. Put the food down for ten minutes; if he doesn't finish, pick it up and put it away until the next meal. Feed a young pup seven to twelve weeks old three times a day, and feed an older puppy or adult dog twice a day. Put the water down at regular intervals and pay attention to how much he drinks. Remember: What goes in comes out.

Don't Punish Your Puppy for Mistakes

An important aspect of housebreaking a dog successfully is to reward success rather than punish mistakes. Mistakes are really your fault for not walking your puppy at the right time. If you'd like to hit yourself over the head with a rolled-up newspaper, feel free! Your puppy will not learn not to go in the house by being scolded or punished. What he will learn is to avoid going in front of you and instead go under the dining room table when no one is looking. The end result is that it will be nearly impossible to get him to go on a leash, because he will come to believe that going in front of someone is wrong.

Deal with mistakes by ignoring the pup for a while. Put him in a crate or gated room, clean up the mess, and make a note of the time of the accident. Keep track of your dog's mistakes to see if there is any pattern to them and if you should add in extra walks.

FACT

If you are not sure you know about all the spots where your dog has gone, consider purchasing a black light (available in some dog supply catalogs) to detect the urine stains on the carpet.

Proper Cleanup Procedures for Accidents

When your puppy has an accident on the carpet or floor, it is essential to clean it up as quickly and as thoroughly as possible to eliminate any lingering odors, because any remaining smell will draw the puppy back to that spot. Here are some tips for cleaning up urine on carpet:

1. Blot up as much as possible with paper towels.
2. Pour an eight-ounce glass of water over the spot to dilute the urine.
3. Blot with more paper towels until there is no hint of yellow on the towels.
4. Spray carpet cleaner over the spot and scrub with a brush or a sponge.
5. Spray the area again and follow the product's directions for standing time and vacuuming. Repeat as needed.
6. Spray with an enzyme inhibitor, which eliminates the odor, following the product directions exactly.

Cleaning up urine or feces on hardwood floors should be done a little differently to prevent permanent damage to the floor.

1. Wipe up excess with paper towels.
2. Add a capful of Murphy Oil soap to a bucket of water and wash the area thoroughly with a mop or sponge.
3. Dry the area thoroughly with a rag or paper towels.
4. Spray an enzyme inhibitor on a cloth and wipe down the area one last time.

Cleaning up feces on carpet can be tricky. Be sure to remove as much as possible with paper towels before treating the area to avoid rubbing the excess into the carpet and thereby compounding the problem.

1. Remove all solid waste with paper towels.
2. Spray with carpet cleaner and rub out as much as possible with a sponge.
3. Spray the area again and use a scrub brush to deep clean the fibers of the carpet.
4. Spray the area with carpet cleaner again and follow the product's directions for standing time and vacuuming. Repeat as needed.
5. Spray with an enzyme inhibitor to permanently eliminate the odor.

Cleaning up accidents efficiently is very important. A dog's sense of smell is intense. If accidents are not cleaned up thoroughly, it can draw the animal back to that spot time and again. Many great products on the market today help clean up the mess and also neutralize the odor, making it less likely that your dog will be drawn back to the same spot.

If your dog tends to continue to go back to the same spot over and over, consider rearranging the furniture a bit to block access to that spot. Cleaning any area where an accident occurred is essential to keeping your dog on track with his housebreaking. If you are cleaning up more than a couple of accidents a week, you are probably not walking your puppy outside often enough or are allowing too much freedom too soon. Remember that limiting a puppy's freedom is half the key to housebreaking and is only temporary until your puppy proves he knows where to "go" and is completely reliable.

Dogs need to go out at least once during a four-hour period if they are confined to a small area such as a crate. If they have more freedom or free access to food and water, they may have to go more frequently. Most house-broken adult dogs need to be walked first thing in the morning, sometime midday, after work, and before bed. A midday visit from a pet sitter can help your adult dog maintain his excellent housebreaking manners.

A lack of housebreaking is a silly reason to give up a dog to the shelter or pound, but living with a dog that uses your house as her bathroom is no picnic either. Housebreaking manners are the most basic of training issues that must be accomplished if a dog is going to live peaceably with humans. The tricks to housebreaking come down to some very basic elements: Confine the dog in some way; put her on a schedule and keep track of her successes and failures; control the food and water bowls; walk her outdoors in short, frequent spurts; and avoid punishing her mistakes. If you follow these guidelines, your dog should make fairly good progress within a month to six weeks.

Occasionally a dog may have a medical problem that interferes with housebreaking. If you were making good progress with housebreaking but your dog suddenly regresses, consider having your veterinarian check a urine and stool sample for signs of infection or parasites. Both of these medical conditions can be easily treated with medication and will often present themselves as a regression in a housebreaking program.

It is not effective to pursue an issue behaviorally if the real problem lies in a medical condition. If, despite your best efforts, you find your dog's housebreaking problems baffling or you adopted your dog late in her life and she came with a host of serious behavioral problems, you may want to consider the help of a professional dog trainer or behaviorist.

CHAPTER 15

Pulling on the Leash

If there is a common problem among dogs, it is pulling on the leash to get where they want to go. From the biggest Great Dane to the tiniest Chihuahua, all dogs regardless of their size learn to pull on their leashes from an early age.

15

The Only Solution Is Training

Leash pulling doesn't seem to be such a big problem until you try to walk around the block with a dog that thinks he's the lead dog in a sled team, determined to reach the dog park in record time. Pulling on the leash is one of the major reasons people stop taking their dogs for walks. It takes all the fun out of a leisurely walk around the neighborhood when one of your arms feels as though it is being pulled out of its socket.

If you look in pet stores and in pet supply catalogs, you will see dozens of devices that supposedly stop your dog from pulling. The truth of the matter, however, is that dogs will continue to pull until you teach them to stop, regardless of the equipment you are using. Only you, as your dog's trusted companion, can choose what method you want to use to teach your dog to walk with you instead of dragging you, and there are many options out there that you can try. The key to any training program, however, is *you*—how much time you invest in the project and how consistent you are about sticking to it until the job is done.

QUESTION?

Why do dogs pull?
Dogs pull because it gets them where they want to go. If every time your dog leaves the house he is allowed to hit the end of the leash and you follow him wherever he pulls you, you are reinforcing the behavior and letting your dog think it is okay.

Define Your Terms

Whenever you want to fix any behavior problem, it is a good idea to sit down and figure out what you would like your dog to do instead. In this case, it is important to define how you want your dog to behave on leash. Do you want him to walk at perfect heel position or is a loose leash sufficient? Where exactly would you like your dog to be, and what will it look like when he's there? Will your arm be relaxed or extended, is sniffing okay, and which side should he be on?

Narrowing down what you are looking for gives you a better idea of what you are going to reinforce and will help you recognize it and reward it. Only by reinforcing the right behavior will you be able to get rid of the undesirable one. If you don't know what your dog has to do to get the reward, you will not be successful at getting rid of pulling and teaching him an acceptable alternative. Sit down with your family now and decide how you want your dog to behave on leash.

A good barometer for heeling is to pay attention to the slack in the leash. Look at the arm that is holding the leash. If your elbow has a bend in it, the dog is walking with you nicely; if your arm is straight, you've got some training to do.

Lack of Exercise Contributes to Pulling

Nowhere is a lack of exercise more apparent than when a dog is on leash. A dog with few outlets for his energy will pull, spin, and tug on leash to get where he wants to go. Giving your dog appropriate outlets for his energy, such as playing with other dogs, swimming, and playing fetch, will help give you a more calm on-leash companion. Active dogs need at least thirty minutes to an hour a day of flat-out running to take the edge off of their energy. Without this outlet you can expect behavior problems. Exercise is part of a dog's basic needs for mental, physical, and emotional stability. To ignore this fact is to set your dog up for failure. If you don't have the time to exercise your dog to the point of fatigue, consider hiring a pet sitter, dog walker, or doggie day care professional to help you give your dog the exercise he needs. Trying to train a dog that is not getting enough exercise is an exercise in frustration and should be avoided at all costs.

Walk Without Pulling

Teaching your dog to walk at your side rather than pull your arm off requires lots of practice and repetition. This is not a behavior that is going to change overnight. Remember that pulling works, or has worked, for quite a long time for most dogs, and behavior that gets reinforced gets repeated. A huge step in the right direction is to stop following the dog when the leash is tight and she's pulling you. This may mean suspending all walks around the block so that she doesn't have the opportunity to practice pulling.

Managing your dog's behavior by not allowing her to practice it isn't teaching her to walk next to you, but it's a step in the right direction since she isn't being reinforced for the wrong behavior. The following are some tips for teaching loose-leash walking:

- Walk at a brisk pace and change direction frequently so that your dog has to pay attention to where you are going. The more turns you offer, the more your dog has to pay attention to where you are.
- Once you get the hang of walking and turning frequently, start to pay attention to the moment your dog turns to follow you, and click and treat her for catching up to you.
- At first, you may want to stop walking for a moment after the click so that the dog realizes what exactly she's getting clicked for. Use really delicious treats that your dog loves to keep her attention focused on you.
- Start off practicing in a distraction-free place, and gradually go to busier places when your dog starts to understand what you want.
- Attaching a six-foot leash to your waist will keep your hands free for this exercise so you will be able to click and treat your dog when she is next to you. Remember that the message you are sending to your dog is that pulling does not get her where she wants to go.
- For most dogs, the faster you walk, the better. A steady pace forces your dog to pay attention to where you are going next.
- Using a clicker to mark the behavior of being next to you will shorten your training time by half. The clicker tells the dog exactly what she's doing right to earn the reward. The clicker is clearer and more precise than any other tool you can use.

When you want to change a behavior that has been working for the dog for quite some time, you need to reinforce the right behavior often and with a high-value reward. Your dog has been pulling to get where she's going for as long as you've had her, so to get rid of pulling you must replace it with a behavior she finds more rewarding. For her to choose to walk next to you over pulling, you will have to do lots of repetitions with yummy rewards.

Really great reinforcements can take the shape of treats like cheese, freeze-dried liver, roast beef, or chicken, or favorite games like tug or fetch. Whatever the reward, the dog has to want it more than she wants to pull. If you are creative and fun, your dog will soon be trotting happily next to you.

Remember that you are building your dog's reinforcement history for loose-leash walking. If you are going to do this effectively, both the rate and value of her rewards have to be high.

Adding the Cue "Heel"

Adding the word "Heel" is the very last thing to do when teaching this behavior. You don't want to label all the pulling and mistakes the dog is making by trying to add the cue in too early. The best time to label the behavior of walking by your side is when the dog is reliably trotting alongside your leg without pulling or stopping. To add the cue, simply say the word "Heel" right before you click and reward. By hearing the word as she moves by your side, your dog will learn to associate (over many repetitions) the behavior of trotting next to you with the word "heel."

Adding Duration to Your Walks

From a training standpoint, duration refers to the amount of time your dog can maintain the requested behavior. In this case, it's the length of time that the dog has to be next to you to earn his click and treat. Once your dog starts to catch on to getting clicked for coming back to your side, you can then raise the criteria to his coming back to your side and staying there for a step or two.

Eventually you will build the length of time the dog must walk next to you to several minutes, until the dog no longer wants to pull. Remember, duration refers to the length of time the dog must do the behavior before he gets rewarded. Practice having him walk with you for different lengths of time around a variety of distractions until he can trot happily next to you under any circumstance.

Changing the Variables and Distractions

Practicing in a new environment—with people, dogs, cars, bicycles, and other distractions—is critical to the reliability of the behavior. Changing too many of these variables at once, however, will make your dog's behavior of walking next to you fall apart. To help your dog to learn to stay with you despite the distractions, change one variable at a time. The variables involved in heeling refer to how close or far you are to the distractions and how intense the distractions are (one person, a crowd, kids, adults, people with dogs, wildlife, cars, bikes, and so forth).

FACT

The length of time you choose should be random so that your dog does not pick up on a pattern. It is probably best not to increase the length of time all at once but instead to skip around with low numbers and then gradually increase the time as the dog catches on to the game.

By controlling the variables and working slowly to introduce distractions while you maintain your dog's ability to walk at heel, you will teach your dog to walk nicely on a leash regardless of the distractions in the environment. Don't ever be afraid to stop the training session and make it easier for the dog to be right if things are going badly and your dog could use some extra help.

Controlling Heeling

There are two major variables involved in teaching your dog to heel: the distance to the distraction and the intensity of the distraction. The distance between your dog and the distraction is too close if you can't get the dog to perform the behavior. If this is the case you should back away from the action to a point where your dog will perform the behavior well. Once your dog is working well, you can decrease the distance between your dog and the distraction, bringing him closer to the action when you are sure he can handle it.

Setting your dog up for success is the key to becoming a good dog trainer. Here are some ways that you can set your dog up for success:

- Reduce the intensity of the distraction (quieter, slower, less of it) as needed.
- Use your best treats; training is difficult, so make it worth his while.
- Offer a high rate of reinforcement in a new environment.
- Slow the rate down (click and treat less frequently) for longer versions of the behavior (dog stays with you longer), and when the dog starts to be able to perform the behavior reliably.

Choose what distraction you will start with and set it up so that your dog can be successful. The intensity of the distraction has to do with its speed, noise level, and quantity. The intensity is too high when your dog can't perform the behavior because he is too distracted. The solution to this problem is to tone down the distraction by making it go slower or quieter or having less of it.

Common Distractions

Another consideration when you are working around distractions with your dog is the type of distraction you are working on. There are three major categories of distractions: things that move, things that smell, and things that make noise. Let's talk about each in turn:

1. **Things that move:** This category incites your dog's prey drive, his desire to chase after things that move. Every dog has a different level of distractibility, but most dogs find things that move irresistible. Examples include cars, bikes, squirrels, runners, dogs, motorcycles, balls, and kids.
2. **Things that smell:** The majority of dogs are motivated most by their stomachs, so for the hunting breeds especially, the "nose to the ground" behavior can be quite a challenge. Examples are food, animals, other animals' feces, and wildlife.
3. **Things that make noise:** Some dogs are more sensitive to sound than others. The average dog is simply curious and will get over it quickly and learn to ignore sounds if you slowly change the variables, distance, and intensity.

Always be sure there isn't a physical reason why your dog won't walk with you. Check his feet for cuts, make sure the pavement isn't too hot, and ensure his feet aren't stinging from salt-treated roads in the wintertime.

Distractions need to be worked into the training gradually. If distractions are too frequent or intense, the dog will get overexcited and be unable to concentrate, and no real learning will occur. It is important that you pay attention to your dog's excitement level and tone down the distractions so that he is able to absorb the lesson.

The Mule Impersonator

Laggards often plant their butts and will not move forward. They will not move or follow you with any amount of coaxing or cooing. You can use several tricks to get these dogs to follow you:

1. Put tension in the lead but don't pull. Make sure the leash is hooked to a regular collar, not a training collar.
2. As soon as your dog takes a step toward you to steady himself, click and treat and lavish with praise. (Some dogs take a while, so be patient.)

3. Repeat this every time your dog stops. Don't go back to him; simply ignore the wrong behavior and pay attention to the right one instead.

4. Within ten minutes or so, most dogs give up their stubborn-mule impression and go with you. Some dogs may need you to do this over several sessions before they give up.

The Bigger the Paycheck, the Less He Will Pull

Teaching your dog to heel can be time consuming and boring—for both of you—if you don't come up with ideas to make it more interesting and fun. One way to make things more fun is to hide the rewards all around your training area before you start your session. It will be such a surprise to the dog to be rewarded with a delicious treat or an awesome toy that she wasn't expecting to be pulled out of the bushes. The element of surprise will make you far more interesting to your dog, and it will make your dog much more willing to learn to walk with you.

Choose Rewards Carefully

A reward is something that causes a behavior to happen again and again. For this to happen, the reward must be something the dog wants. Spend some time to find out what motivates your dog—what type of treats she likes, what toys she likes, what games she likes. All of these can be used as a reward for walking next to you rather than pulling you. Remember that your dog might not like all the things she finds rewarding in all environments. For instance, she may love to work for her dry dog food when practicing walking without pulling in a quiet environment, but she may turn her nose up at it when she is working outside or in a busy environment like a pet store or veterinary office.

Many new trainers are amazed when their dogs turn their noses up at what they perceive as a really good treat (like cheese or a piece of hot dog) in a new environment. Finding the treats you need to use in distracting environments to keep your dog working and focused on you is challenging, but it is the only way to ensure progress and success. Knowing ahead of time what treats work where or what toys/games work in what environments will help you achieve your goals without frustration. It is worthwhile to make a list of treats, toys, and games and rank them for your dog by environment. Knowing that you can get away with using dog food in training sessions around the house but need cheese or liver when working outdoors is valuable information that will save you time. When you take the time to train your dog, you want to make progress with the lesson instead of fumbling for a reinforcer that the dog will work for.

QUESTION?

Can scared dogs learn to ignore new sounds and walk at heel?
You can train any dog to walk at heel. For the scared dog, it would be best to teach her to deal with novel noises and build her confidence first. Once she loses his skittishness, then try to teach her to heel around such distractions.

You may also want to consider using a variety of rewards paired with the click. Some examples are a game of tug, a game of fetch, a stuffed toy, a fantastic belly or flank rub, and lots of excited praise. You can teach your dog that you are interesting and full of great surprises by hiding your goodies everywhere and keeping your dog guessing about what you're going to pull out next.

Training Equipment

Training collars, head halters, and other devices are just that: devices. Their purpose is to manage pulling while you are teaching your dog to heel. The goal should be to have your dog learn to heel with the help of a training device and then to wean the dog off that device and have her heel without it.

Collars

You can find several training devices that keep dogs from pulling. The most common are the regular slip collar or choke chain, the pinch collar, and the head halter. A slip collar works by restricting the dog's airway for a fraction of a second and making it unpleasant for him to pull. A pinch collar works by pinching the skin around the dog's neck and making it unpleasant to pull. A head halter works by pulling the dog's head downward, making it impossible to walk until the dog stops pulling and walks closer to the handler.

As with any device, you must teach your dog the step-by-step process for heeling, and in most cases this should occur before you start using the device itself. After the dog has learned how to get rewarded, the use of a training device will help you sort out the various distractions. Special situations, such as the veterinary clinic, may require extra management before your dog is completely trained. No one device is right for every dog, but the head halter is probably the most useful for most dogs.

ALERT!

No device will "teach" your dog to heel. You are the one who must break down this leash-walking issue into simple steps that you can incorporate into training a little at a time. The training devices will help you manage behavior, but that is all.

Head Halter Benefits

One particular name brand of head halter, the Gentle Leader Headcollar, tends to fit better than others available on the market today. It has two adjustable straps: one for the neck and one for the muzzle. The leash clips underneath the dog's chin. Think of the way a halter on a horse fits and you'll have an idea of how this works. The head halter controls the dog's forward movement by controlling the dog's head, which gives it an advantage over the other types of training equipment. You would never expect to move a horse by pulling on its neck, for instance, but you can easily move a 1,200-pound animal in the direction you want to go by guiding it by its head—well, at least most of the time!

This same principle works for dogs. The head halter is not a muzzle. The dog can still eat, catch a ball, and bite with it on, and no dog should be left unattended while wearing it. If your dog should try to bite or eat something he shouldn't while wearing the head halter, you can easily close his mouth by gently pulling up on the leash. The pressure that exerts will easily close the dog's mouth and pull his head down, effectively preventing him from continuing the behavior. The head halter is sometimes described as self-correcting, meaning the handler does not have to pull on the leash or yank the dog in any way to get him to stop what he is doing. It is also important to note that if you choose to use this device, you should attach only a six-foot leash to it, never an extendable or retractable one. If your dog were to take off after something and hit the end of a long leash while wearing a head halter, he could injure his neck. Introduce the head halter over a period of about two weeks. The longer you take to make this fun for the dog, the more useful a training tool it will be.

The introduction of the head halter should be a gradual process, whereby you slowly teach the dog that wearing it is fun and means good stuff is about to happen. Your goal is to make the dog as excited to see the head halter as he is to see his leash. Using a clicker and the yummiest treats, introduce the head halter by following these steps:

1. Show the halter to your dog and click and treat him for sniffing at it.
2. Open the nose loop and click and treat your dog for poking his nose through it to get at the treat.
3. Once he's eagerly putting his nose through the loop on his own, give him a good-sized treat and fasten the neck strap while he's chewing.
4. Let him move around a bit and click and treat him for not pawing at his nose.
5. If your dog gets the nose loop off, take the whole thing off and leave him alone for ten minutes or so. Completely ignoring him will make him all the more eager to work with you again. The idea here is that he will want to keep the halter on because you pay extra attention to him and give special treats only when he has it on.
6. Later, when he isn't pawing as much, attach a leash to the clip under the chin and repeat steps 4 and 5. You will have to go back and click and treat him for walking without pawing at his face every time you intro-duce a new distraction or variable.
7. You are now ready to use the head halter on your walks, but go slowly. Take your dog for a short walk, and click and treat him for walking

outside without pawing at his face. Keep the walk to no more than five minutes.

8. As your dog gets used to wearing the head halter in public, you can gradually increase the distractions, the length of time you walk him, and any of the other variables.

Remember to make it easy for the dog to be right if you notice any regression around distractions. This is especially common when other dogs are present. The head halter can be a wonderful tool for helping you manage your dog around distractions and teaching him not to pull, but introducing it takes time, so don't rush your dog.

ALERT!

Think of the head halter as a guide. Use it to guide your dog on his walks. Never pull, snap, or correct your dog in the halter, as it could damage his neck or spine. Be patient when introducing your dog to the head halter. Many dogs find the sensation of having something around their nose strange, and they may resist at first.

If this device isn't useful for a dog, it is usually because the owner rushed the introduction because the dog seemed to tolerate it fairly well. Don't be fooled—just like with training other things, you get out what you put in. The following are tips for making this work for you:

- Be patient during this introduction. The head halter is a more useful tool if you introduce it slowly and let the dog learn to like wearing it (up to a week or two).
- You will have no need for jerks or pops or corrections with a head halter; in fact, doing so can injure a dog's neck or spine.
- Make sure you read the halter's directions carefully before you use it on your dog. It's important that you teach your dog to wear it and avoid letting him lunge or pull while wearing it. Lunging or pulling can injure your dog's neck or spine, causing him discomfort and long-term medical problems.
- If you have trouble, find a qualified positive trainer to help you introduce this piece of equipment to your dog.

Body Harnesses

Easy Walk or Sense-sation harnesses are designed to keep a dog from pulling, and they work very well for most dogs. The nice thing about this piece of equipment is that there is little to no introduction. You just fit the harness to the dog and off you go. The harness is specially designed to keep the dog from pulling by changing his center of gravity if he puts his weight forward. The clip for the leash goes on the front ring of the harness, which helps the dog notice this effect. A good fit is essential for the proper use of the harness, but this is a good alternative tool for a determined puller.

CHAPTER 16

Lunging and
On-Leash Aggression

Dog aggression sometimes gets its start from inappropriate leash manners in a young dog. Adult dogs find it rude when an adolescent dog jumps on them or gets in their space uninvited. The human end of the leash often makes the problem worse by making the leash too short and not paying attention to what the dog is doing.

Leashes Can Cause Aggressive Behavior

When dogs are off leash and encounter other dogs or stimuli, they are free to get away, display a "don't bother me" attitude, or simply invite the other dog to play. Dogs on leash cannot show these same emotions, and they feel more cornered and threatened. Leashes and the owners who hold them can make it impossible for dogs to give the appropriate signals to each other and tend to get in the way of communicating rather than helping the dogs get along. Dog owners who fear their dog's reaction to other dogs often don't help matters because they tense up and tighten the leash, signaling to the dog that trouble lies ahead.

People with on-leash dogs tend to approach each other head-on, whereas dogs normally approach one another in a curved half circle. Approaching head-to-head is a combative signal that says you mean business and may want to fight. Your dog may recognize another dog's rank and lower himself ever so slightly to signal to the other dog that he means no harm. As a human, however, you pull yourself and the leash upright when you see the other dog coming. Pulling up on the leash changes your dog's body posture into a more threatening stance, causing the other dog to react and your dog to become defensive. The higher-ranking dog is taken by surprise and attacks your dog for changing his mind and posturing the wrong message at the last moment. No wonder it is difficult for on-leash dogs to get along!

Bad Leash Manners Get Dogs into Trouble

Teaching your dog how he is supposed to behave on leash around other dogs is a crucial skill that will keep him safe and out of trouble. Many dogs who have had some socialization with other dogs but are aggressive on their leashes have not learned the skills they need to negotiate the world. Because of this, they get themselves into trouble around other dogs. In general, good leash manners involve staying with the handler until given permission to greet another dog. It is a dog's job to stay close to his owner whether walking on a loose leash or holding a Sit or Down/Stay so that the handlers can walk by each other in peace. Not every dog wants to be greeted by another dog, and most dogs take offense to being jumped upon.

In dogspeak it is rude to go right up to another dog, put your paws on her, and mouth her or otherwise jump on or harass her. Most adult dogs with good social skills have little tolerance for these behaviors from puppies and adolescent dogs, and the correction they give, though appropriate, is often misinterpreted by the other dog, who may become frightened and even aggressive toward other dogs on leash.

As the handler, it is worthwhile to realize that not all dogs like all other dogs and that doesn't make them aggressive. Being able to walk down the street with your handler and ignore other dogs on leash is the ideal. Play-dates where the dogs can be off leash to run and play and wrestle is the ideal way for dogs to socialize. When they are on leash, it's all business.

QUESTION?

What should I do when my dog greets another dog on leash?
It is crucial to keep a loose leash when allowing your dog to greet another dog on leash. Always ask first to make sure the other dog is normally friendly and let the dogs approach each other from the side rather than the front.

The person holding the leash is often the one responsible for the greeting going badly, as he inadvertently pulls the dog into a more dominant posture, which sends exactly the wrong message to the other dog. The source of the problem comes down to poor leash manners on the dog's part and not enough control on the owner's part.

Dog Manners

Dogs that launch themselves at other on-leash dogs in play are also sending the wrong message. Jumping on other dogs that are trapped on leash and can't get away is rude and bad dog manners. Dogs that do this are often corrected sharply by other dogs, and their owners often mistake this for true aggression. If this scenario is repeated enough, the friendly dog starts to learn to be defensive, sowing the seeds for future leash aggression. The reality here is that the jumping dog has poor leash manners and broke a cardinal rule: No jumping on an adult dog.

No on-leash dog should have to put up with another dog jumping on him, even in play. It is important as the owner to make sure that you have appropriate control of your dog around other dogs. The more well trained your dog is, the better accepted he will be by other on-leash dogs, and people as well. Too many bad experiences will make the dog wary of approaching other dogs on leash and cause reflexive, defensive aggression.

Leash manners for well-socialized dogs include not pulling or lunging around other dogs, sitting when greeting another dog and owner, and only going to other dogs with permission. Cultivating these manners is up to the one who wields the leash—the owner.

The Leash

The best type of leash for walking an aggressive dog is a six-foot nylon or leather leash. A dog with lunging and aggression problems should not be on an extendable leash, nor should she ever be off leash around other dogs. A six-foot leash allows you to control your dog and keep her close to you. The way you hold the leash is important to your dog's progress as well. In general, it is best to hold it with two hands, one hand through the loop end and the other about halfway down the length. This allows your dog a little slack but not so much that she can lunge ahead of you without you being able to easily prevent it. Holding the leash too tightly so that your dog has barely enough room to move is not recommended.

Don't force your dog to walk right next to you; let her have a little slack. The slacker the leash is, the less confined and cornered she will feel when she sees another dog, but don't let her get too far away from you. When the leash is attached to a Gentle Leader Headcollar, remember that it is self-correcting and does not require you to jerk or pull. If your dog tries to lunge, the action will naturally pull her head to the ground. Before your dog lunges, you should try to get her attention back on you and move in the opposite direction. Make sure you are prepared to move away from the other dog, and also to click and treat your dog for moving with you. Throwing the reward on the ground is also a good idea, because it may be a little more interesting for your dog, giving you the time you need to get her under control while the other dog goes on its way.

ALERT!

The way you hold the leash is an important part of successful dog interactions. The looser the leash, the better able your dog is to show other dogs that she means no harm. Maintaining slack in the leash will enable your dog to discriminate friendly dogs from not-so-friendly ones. Many behavior problems started with a leash that was too tight and a dog with no leash manners.

Leash Manners

For dogs with good social skills that get into trouble when on leash, take some simple steps to help improve on-leash manners. First of all, you need to use the right equipment. There are lots of products on the market today that help you to control your dog's pulling. The problem with these devices is that they fool you into thinking your dog knows not to pull on his leash, but the dog goes back to pulling as soon as the device is removed. The important thing to keep in mind is that all training collars and devices are just that, devices. They facilitate training; they do not replace it. Regardless of what piece of training equipment you use, you must click and treat your dog for not pulling and eventually label it and wean the dog off the treats, clicker, and the collar.

Many people make the mistake of using training collars on dogs without explaining to the dog what the device is meant to do. When using a training collar, you must reward the dog for walking with you, or the dog will have no idea what is expected of him. With a training collar, when the dog pulls, the handler jerks and releases the leash to make pulling an unpleasant choice. The dog is supposed to stop pulling (at least for a second). You must then reward the dog when he stops pulling, or no real learning will occur. If you don't reward your dog for the right behavior, you will not get the right behavior.

Most dogs that are not rewarded for the appropriate behavior end up thinking the exercise is "run to the end of the leash, your owner gives you a yank, go back to her side, and run to the end of the leash again." Not all dogs will respond this way, however. Some very sensitive dogs will fall apart the first time they are corrected and never try to pull again, but they are doing so out of fear, not because they have learned that you want them next to you. Sensitive dogs should probably not wear training collars in the first place since they learn quickly through much gentler methods, such as a head halter.

The head halter (see Chapter 15) works very well while training your dog not to pull. The leash clip is under the dog's chin so there is no constriction of the windpipe when the dog pulls. These collars are also self-correcting. When the dog pulls forward, the head is forced down, effectively stopping the dog from moving forward. This means that there is no need to jerk on the leash or correct your dog; in fact, doing so may damage his neck. The head halter teaches a dog not to pull by operating on several principles:

1. A dog that pulls while wearing a head halter ends up with his nose to the ground and cannot walk forward until he puts slack in the leash.
2. Since the halter fits over the dog's neck and muzzle, it gives the handler complete control over the dog's head.
3. If you control where the head goes, the body must follow.
4. The way the collar fits (over the back of the neck and over the top of the muzzle) mimics what a mother dog does when she disciplines her pups.
5. Because the owner now has complete control, many dogs learn to trust their handlers and pay more attention to them.

The head halter is a must for teaching on-leash manners. When used correctly, this device will prevent lunging, and it will also lower the dog's head and body carriage, which will make her less likely to provoke other dogs. The simple fact that you now control the dog's head is enough to prevent problems in the future.

Reward the Right Behavior

Teach your dog to be polite on leash around other dogs by clicking and treating her for approaching dogs sideways instead of head-on, for turning her head away instead of staring, and for offering a play Bow instead of jumping on the other dog. The play bow, a natural behavior in which the dog puts her chest and belly close to the ground and her fanny in the air, is a behavior you can put on cue so that you can ask your dog to Bow when greeting another dog.

A dog that isn't getting enough exercise is sure to be obnoxious on leash. Her built-up energy has to come out somehow and will manifest itself in lunging, leaping, and frantic on-leash behavior. If this describes your dog, provide more exercise and outlets for her pent-up energy and exuberance for life.

Remember that when teaching a dog to heel on leash, the most important point is not to follow a dog that is pulling. When your dog pulls and you follow, you are reinforcing your dog for pulling to get where she wants to go. If your dog is a few years old, she probably already has a substantial bank account for pulling and lunging, and you will have some training to do if you are going to compete with that. The first step is to make lots of turns so that you are always in the lead and your dog has to closely watch you to see where you are going to end up next. Changing direction and clicking and treating your dog for catching up is the key to teaching your dog that being next to you is better than pulling or lagging behind. With lots of repetition and changes in variables and distractions, your dog will start to understand that walking on leash means walking next to you, not yanking you down the street.

Teach Your Dog to Leave It

Leave It means that the dog stops and looks back at his handler. This definition will help you in many situations, from your dog chasing a cat or squirrel across a busy street to lunging at another dog or person. Leave It means "stop what you are doing or thinking about doing and look in my direction." Once your dog is looking at you, you have a much greater chance of getting him to respond to your directions to Heel, Come, Lie Down, or whatever. Teaching your dog to Leave It is probably the most important thing your dog must learn if he is going to be safe to walk in public places. The faster and more reliable response to this behavior, the better your control will be.

For dogs that lack social skills, training your dog to Leave It will be your best management tool. The longer your dog can look at you, the better able you will be to control him around other dogs and people. Leave It is an invaluable command for dogs that lunge at other dogs on leash. When teaching Leave It, it is important to catch the dog before he starts to lunge and bark. Once the dog is barking and lunging, he is no longer in learning mode, and no amount of yelling or corrections will get him there. You must beat him to this highly charged emotional state by interrupting him before he really notices the other dog and then reversing direction so that he moves with you. Click and treat your dog for moving away from the other dog and going with you.

One way to increase your dog's enthusiasm for turning away is to throw a whole handful of treats in the grass so that he has to hunt for them. The time it takes for him to do this will give the other dog and owner time to go by you. When your dog is finished, you can continue on your walk.

Because following you and leaving the distraction is a new pattern of behavior, you'll have to practice it over and over until your dog does it almost automatically. With enough repetition he may even start to offer the behavior on his own. If your timing is off and you don't turn your dog in time, he will explode into a frenzy of barking. There is nothing you can do at this point except just get through it and try again the next time. At the very least, by not yelling at or correcting the dog you will not reinforce the undesirable behavior.

Here are the steps to teaching your dog to leave another dog:

1. Use familiar dogs at first so that you can completely control your training session and the dogs. Have your helper and distraction dog start on the opposite side of the street.
2. Make sure you interrupt your dog when he's thinking about lunging or barking. Interrupt him by saying his name and then turning 180 degrees in the opposite direction. Click and treat him for turning with you.
3. If your dog doesn't turn with you, it means that you are too close to the distraction dog; move away from the other dog by a couple of more feet and try again.
4. Throw a whole handful of goodies for your dog to clean up after you click so that you make it well worth his while to pay attention to you.
5. Once your dog is ignoring the other dog and turning with you easily, shorten the distance by having the dog approach on the same side of the street and repeat from the start.
6. Build up to being able to have the distraction dog pass within several feet with no reaction from your dog.
7. Change the distractions by using different dogs and changing where you practice until your dog can ignore any dog anywhere. When the dog is easily turning away from other dogs for a click and treat, label the head turn Leave It right before the dog turns his head.

For training purposes, the distraction dog should be a completely reliable well-socialized adult dog that will not react to your dog in any way. It will also help to have the distraction dog wear a head halter to help your dog perceive him as nonthreatening. Vary the scenarios until your dog is eagerly looking to you when he sees other dogs.

Set Reasonable Goals

Dogs with few social skills are never going to be totally friendly or trustworthy with other dogs. You can't resocialize an adult dog that has no experience with other dogs. Doing so would be dangerous and most likely end in injury to dogs or the humans. The best that can be done with dogs like this is to set a reasonable goal. Your goal might be to have your dog like other dogs, but a more reasonable goal might be to have him respond immediately to your command to Leave It.

Teaching your dog appropriate leash manners of not lunging or barking and turning his head away from other dogs rather than staring them down will mean you can take him more places and be able to control him. Acknowledge that though you would like your dog to get along with other dogs, your dog is perfectly content to not have any contact with them. Don't force your own desire for your dog to have friends on him; he may feel he has as many friends as she needs, and no amount of pushing on your part will change that. Respect what your dog is trying to tell you and keep him safe around other dogs.

If you have a young puppy, let him meet and play with as many different kinds of puppies and adult dogs as you can. The window for socializing a dog to other dogs is short—between seven and eighteen weeks. As the window closes, your dog is less open to new experiences and less likely to be social with other dogs.

Make the Commitment

The worst thing you can do with this type of problem is to rush. Your dog did not get this way overnight, and no one thing you do is going to magically change your dog's opinion of other dogs. This process of teaching appropriate manners to a dog with no social experience is time consuming. You must be totally committed to helping improve your dog's behavior in order to even put a dent in the problem. A halfhearted attempt to change your dog's behavior will not help you reach your goal. To make progress, you will have to do hundreds of repetitions of Leave It and put lots of time into practicing keeping the leash loose. This is a long-term program; don't expect miracles overnight. As with anything in life, you get out of it what you put into it. If you practice diligently and set reasonable goals, you will eventually be rewarded by a more enjoyable walking companion.

The Bar Is Open

Classical conditioning can be a very powerful tool in getting faster and more reliable results in your training program. The Bar Is Open, the Bar Is Closed technique uses the principles of classical conditioning to change the way your dog feels about other dogs on leash. Classical conditioning deals with associations (see Chapter 13). The presence of other dogs means that the bar is open and all kinds of good things happen, including affection, attention, and treats, regardless of the dog's behavior. She can be lunging or barking hysterically and you continue to drop treats like it is her birthday. When the other dog disappears, so do the treats and games and attention; in fact, the handler gives the dog the outright cold shoulder.

When using classical conditioning to change your dog's behavior, you'll want to be sure you keep your distance so that the other dogs can't come right up to you. Be sure your dog is on leash and at enough of a distance so as to give her every opportunity for success.

Classical conditioning tries to change the way a dog feels about having other dogs around by associating other dogs with good things. The drawback of this technique is that it takes the animal time to realize the association between the good stuff and the offending presence of another dog. The way to use this technique effectively is to practice frequently to give your dog an increasingly big bank account for liking the sight of other dogs.

Eventually your dog will like having other dogs around because it means she is going to have access to all the things she loves.

Here's how it works in real life:

1. Choose a spot where other dogs are likely to pass by. Bring all of your very best reinforcements. This can range from cheese, liver, and hot dogs to tennis balls, tug toys, and squeaky toys.
2. When other dogs are within sight, regardless of your dog's behavior, the bar is open. You bounce the ball, throw it, roll it, and shower your dog with treats, toys, and attention. As soon as the dog is out of sight, the bar is closed. You put your goodies away, step on the leash, and ignore your dog completely for at least two minutes.
3. When another dog comes by, you again open the bar; when it disappears, close the bar.
4. After repeating this over and over again, your dog will learn a new reaction to other dogs. She will learn that when other dogs are present, good things happen, and when they go, the fun is over.

Lunging and on-leash aggression are fairly serious behavior problems that require lots of consistent practice to change. These behaviors will not go away with just a little training, and good leash behavior needs to be constantly maintained. Dogs revert back to old habits if you don't consistently reinforce the right behaviors. Consider this behavior problem one that needs constant maintenance to ensure that the dog adopts the new behavior as a habit.

Remember that bad habits are hard to get rid of because they are comfortable. (Think of eating the wrong foods or smoking.) If a new behavior is going to replace an old one, there must be some planning involved and time set aside for practice. Keep in mind that as with any old habit, there will be regression and mistakes. Plan for them so they don't derail you and you can easily get back on track. With time, patience, love, and training, you can make any dog a better companion.

CHAPTER 17

Running Away

Dogs that don't come when they are called have learned that getting away from you is rewardable. When the average person calls her dog, she puts the leash back on and goes home, crates the dog and goes to work, or puts the dog in the car and drives away. Since it normally isn't beneficial for the dog to come, the dog chooses to reward herself and run away. If the dog runs off and finds things to eat, roll in, and play with, then running away has huge benefits.

Use a Leash to Control the Variables

The most important thing to remember is that every time your dog takes off and has a good time he is putting money in his bank account for not coming back. Don't allow an untrained dog off leash in an unsafe area or an area where he will be difficult to catch. A dog that has an unreliable recall is a danger to himself. He doesn't have good judgment and may run into the street, get lost, or eat something harmful. If you love your dog, use a leash in unfenced areas so that you do not give your dog the opportunity to run away.

FACT

When you use a leash to teach your dog to come, you are using it to limit his options. The fewer options he has, the more likely he is to be right and choose coming to you over running away to please himself.

Keeping your dog on leash gives him the ability to be right more often and allows you to reinforce those choices, making it likely he will choose you again and again. When you eventually get to the point where you are not using a leash anymore, it will be easy to get rid of it and still have the same level of behavior. Since you have used the leash to teach him to come by limiting his options rather than yanking on it, you have made it more likely that he will choose you over distractions.

Puppies aged nine to twelve weeks are usually too unsure of themselves to wander far if you let them off leash. If your confident puppy strays too far, play hide and seek with him by hiding behind a tree and calling "puppy, puppy" in a high pitched voice. Most puppies can't resist this and will come looking for you, giving you an opportunity to reward this behavior.

Make the Rewards Worth the Effort

Your dog needs you to use the best possible rewards if he's going to choose coming to you over pursuing a distraction. Remember that a squirrel, cat, child, or another dog is a thrill to chase, bark at, or sniff around. If your dog chooses to be with you over the distraction, make sure you have the best treats, toys, or games as the reward. You will mark your dog's behavior of turning in your direction with a click and follow it with a treat, a game, or an opportunity to interact with the distraction (but only after checking in with you first). Using rewards in this way is not a bribe; you are simply requiring that your dog check in with you before he gets what he wants. For dogs that learn this game, it almost completely eliminates the desire to run away. Using rewards in this way means you control the dog's access to what he wants and you pay up when he checks in with you.

The best way to use a nonfood reward is to limit the time you interact with the dog after the click to a few seconds if it's a game, or use the real-life reward at the end of the session as a way to reinforce to the dog that coming to you is just the most terrific thing ever.

Ideas for Rewards

Making the rewards variable and exciting will enhance your dog's performance and make the process of teaching your dog to come all the more fun. Here are some things to keep in mind when you are considering different types of rewards in your training program:

- **Food rewards** can include cheese, liver, chicken, beef jerky, tortellini, hot dogs, roast beef, and steak.
- **Toy rewards** can include stuffed animals, balls, tug toys, and Frisbees.
- **Game rewards** such as fetch, tug, and Frisbee can help a high-energy dog stay focused on you and redirect the energy that would have been used to chase the distraction.
- **Real-life rewards** include the opportunity to chase the distraction (a ball, a squirrel, a leaf), to say hello to the person or other dog, to play with the group of dogs off leash, to swim in the pond, to plow through the snow, or to roll in the smell.

Leadership Matters

Ninety percent of a dog's recall has to do with who's in charge. Dogs with firm, strong leaders almost always come when called because you are in charge of everything great and your judgment is worth trusting. Being a leader in no way implies being a bully or making your dog do something; in fact, true leaders never have to force a dog to do anything. Leadership is about setting limits and having rules about what is allowed and what is not. Having guidelines is essential if your dog is going to do as you wish.

When you require that your dog earn privileges, you are in charge. When the dog gets them for free, she doesn't need you and won't trust your judgment. Controlling whatever it is that the dog wants is the key to controlling the dog's behavior.

Quite simply, a strong leader controls resources that the dog wants access to, including her dinner, the outdoors, attention and affection, and space (including sleeping places). In a nutshell, leadership entails being first, being more powerful, and being in charge. Your ideas and decisions rule, not the dog's.

Being the leader means you control the resources the dog wants. It does not mean, under any circumstances, that you dominate or bully the dog in any way. Here are some guidelines for you to review:

- **Nothing in life is free.** Your dog must do something to get something.
- **Respond quickly to commands.** Pick a number of seconds that you'll give your dog to respond to the command; if she doesn't respond on the first command within the time frame you've chosen, she doesn't get whatever you were about to give her.
- **No dogs on your bed.** No dog, let alone a dog with a behavior problem (especially a recall problem), should be allowed to sleep on the highest, most privileged spot in the house: your bed.
- **Leaders go first through doorways and up and down stairs**. Teach your dog to wait and let you go first.

- **No dogs on the furniture;** your dog should be on the floor or in her crate or bed.
- **Leaders control space and move about without interference.** Don't step over or around your dog; if she's in your way, make her move.
- **Leaders initiate attention and games.** Pushy dogs that hound you with toys or nudging should be ignored until they give up. You can call them to you later when it's your idea to play.

ALERT!

If you are strict at first, you can relax your rules later and allow your dog privileges without losing ground. Having rules is essential for a dog that is content and relaxed. Just like children, dogs take comfort in the fact that someone else is in charge so that they can enjoy just being dogs.

You, as the leader, can control what your dog wants by controlling her options and what she's allowed to have. The rule is that when you are experiencing behavior problems, you need to be strict about allowing privileges and having house rules. When your dog behaves in a more acceptable way in a few months' time, you can relax some of the rules here and there without losing your status as leader. Think of it as similar to allowing a child to stay up later in the summertime. Staying up later in the summer is a special thing for a child; once September comes, she knows she will have to go to bed at the usual time.

Building a Foundation for Come

The foundation for Come is the most important part of the exercise. It requires that your dog turn away from the distraction and look back at you (and eventually move toward you as well). The Come command is really a Leave It command, because the dog has to turn away from what he wants and come back to you. The more reliable your dog is about turning away from the things he wants, the better able you will be to get her to come to you anytime, anyplace.

If you teach a strong foundation for self-control (see Chapter 9), Come will be easier to train, and your dog will be reliable anywhere you take her. Although you have already taught Come to your dog (see Chapter 5), take a moment to review the shaping steps again:

1. Stand with your dog on a leash and don't let her get to what she wants; when your dog turns away from what she wants and looks back at you, click and treat.
2. If it takes your dog more than a minute to look back, you are too close to the distraction; back away.
3. When the dog is turning in your direction easily, run backward as she turns to look at you and let her catch you. Click your dog as she is moving toward you and put the treat at your feet.
4. Practice putting the treat between your feet, so when she takes it, it will be easier for you to catch her.
5. Practice handling your dog's collar and leading her by it, clicking and treating her for tolerating being led by it.
6. Label the behavior Come when you have the dog by the collar.
7. Change the environment and distractions, practicing in various places.
8. Use a longer leash, twelve to twenty-five feet, and repeat from the beginning.
9. Let your leash drag until your dog proves he understands the command.
10. Vary the size and type of rewards to keep the dog guessing as to what he'll get.

QUESTION?

How can I speed up my dog's response to Come?
Using a reward that your dog really likes can make the difficult task of coming when called more fun and rewarding for the dog. Experiment with different types of food, toys, games, and opportunities and see how it affects your dog's performance.

Change Old Patterns

Old habits die hard, and a dog that consistently runs away to entertain himself is practicing the very opposite of the behavior you are trying to teach him. If your dog has run away a lot in the past and gotten away with rewarding himself again and again, you are going to have to put in a lot of time to prevent him from running away and reward him for coming with really memorable rewards.

Don't miss opportunities to reward your dog for good behavior. Even if you are not directly training your dog to Come, reward your dog for any amount of checking in with you. This in and of itself sometimes is enough to get the check-in behavior started.

Some dogs refuse to come to you because nothing good happens when they do. For instance, just before you leave for work, you call your dog in from the yard, put him in his crate, and leave him there for eight hours. At the park, you call him away from his dog friends and then put him in the car and go home. Try to change this setup by calling him several times before you actually need to leave and allow him to go back to playing as the reward. Changing your pattern of behavior (calling the dog and putting him back on leash, for instance) may be harder than you think.

Again, having a plan of action—what you desire and what you will reward—will make training easier. Prepare ahead of time how you are going to react, and you will be rewarded by a dog that is much more likely to come to you than run away and reward himself.

Keep Recall Positive

Punishment only stops the undesirable behavior; it doesn't teach the dog anything. By the time you've punished your dog for running away, you have him back. In his mind, you are punishing him for coming to you, making it unlikely that you'll get him to respond enthusiastically in the future.

Remote punishment through the use of electronic collars is also not appropriate in the hands of the average pet owner. Even when used by professionals, such devices can teach the dog to be distrustful and fearful of his environment. It is much safer and more reasonable to teach your dog what you expect of him and avoid punishment altogether. When it comes right down to it, punishment misses the point; it is almost always issued too late to be instructive and if it isn't delivered with perfect timing, it will have absolutely no positive effect on the dog's behavior. Use your time and energy wisely. Teach the dog what is expected of him instead of punishing him for making a mistake.

FACT

Teaching your dog that the consequences for coming when called are good is the best way to have a reliable recall. A good consequence could be a few minutes of attention and affection from you, a really good treat or game, or the opportunity to go right back to what you called him away from.

An Ounce of Prevention

In addition to proper training, you can ensure that your dog will come back to you by making sure she is well exercised and well supervised.

The Importance of Exercise

The more exercise your dog gets, the more likely she will be to come back when you call her. A dog with no opportunity to run and explore will be less likely to return to you on demand. Make sure your dog gets to play and run for at least thirty minutes to an hour every day. Ideally, she should exercise and wrestle with other dogs; if interactive play isn't possible, chasing a ball, swimming, or other energy-expending pursuits are a must.

If there is an easy way to put a dent in the solving of a behavioral problem, this is it. Almost any professional dog trainer will tell you that a tired dog is a good dog! Backyard confinement doesn't count. Most dogs don't want to be by themselves, and without a companion they will often bark, howl, chew, and escape the confines of their yard. Meaningful interaction is the key to engaging the dog's mind and body and making sure that her needs for exercise are met.

Play hide-and-seek with your whole family and take turns letting the dog find you. Call her back and forth to you in the yard, in a big field, or at the beach (have her drag a long leash if you think she'll take off). Play fetch, blow bubbles for her to chase and catch, or take her swimming. Whatever activities you choose, get out and get active and enjoy your dog and the great outdoors.

Consider this: The more time you spend exercising your dog, the better you'll feel, too! All levels of the relationship between family and pet benefit from the time you spend together. If you combine your daily workout with exercise for your dog, you'll both be happier and healthier.

The Importance of Supervision

If you are not there, you cannot fix a problem. This is obviously stated but often forgotten when dog owners are trying to fix behavior that has a long history of being reinforced in the wrong direction. If your dog runs away on a regular basis, chances are you have your work cut out for you in finding enough motivation for the dog to come back to you. For instance, if a dog slips out the front door and runs around the neighborhood eating trash, digging up lawns, and chasing bunnies, chances are she has found this very reinforcing. If it happens often enough, it becomes a very tough habit to break.

Remember that consequences drive behavior and if we want a dog to come to us when we call, we need to not only have reinforced her for it hundreds of times, but also have a way to prevent her from rewarding herself for the wrong behavior. Prevention is the key to success. In this case, the less opportunity the dog has to tour the neighborhood, the more likely she is to want to come to us when we call him. Supervise your dog and use a leash, gates, crates, or fences to prevent her from getting reinforced for the behaviors you don't want. Put your time into training and reinforcing her for the things you do want and you will have a dog that stays close and comes when you call her.

The difference between a trained dog that comes when called and an untrained dog that doesn't is based on the dog's perception of who controls what he wants. Dogs behave in ways that benefit them, so the key to having a dog that is always willing to come when called is making it worth the dog's while, regardless of the distraction.

Safe Confinement

You can confine your dog any number of ways, but it's important to pay careful attention to details so that he can't escape. Keep in mind that no dog should be left unsupervised outdoors unless you have an absolutely escape-proof, locked, chain link run. You can call a fence company to come and design a dog pen to fit your needs, but keep in mind that dogs that are confined outdoors tend to develop barking problems.

A Homemade Pen

If you build your own pen, you must keep several things in mind during design and construction. Ideally, you should bury ¼-inch mesh wire about three to four inches under a gravel base; if your dog decides to dig, he can't dig out. Watch your dog carefully to make sure he doesn't eat the gravel. Consider several options for the bottom surface of the pen. A cement slab may be a good choice if there is adequate shade, but it is not the most comfortable surface to lie on in extreme weather conditions. One very effective solution is concrete patio block (or pavers) surrounded by crushed stone. The size of the stone can be whatever you feel would be best for your dog.

Depending on the size of your dog pen, you could put some kind of dog-house or shelter at one end, use patio block for half the length, and leave the rest just plain stone. This arrangement makes it easier to disinfect the pen, keeps the smell to a minimum, and is attractive to look at. A locked gate is essential to prevent anyone from stealing your dog. It is not a good idea to leave your dog unattended, but in circumstances where you need to be gone for an extended period, a pen will at least give your dog a chance to relieve himself in an appropriate place.

Your first job is to teach your dog that looking back at you is the best way to gain access to the things he wants. If he has this basic foundation, your chances for a successful recall will be greater.

Invisible Fences

An invisible fence is a buried wire around the perimeter of your property that provides an electrical barrier that discourages your dog from leaving your yard. To keep your dog within the confines of the yard, your dog wears a collar that gives him an electrical correction if he crosses the barrier. The biggest problem with these fences is that they do not prevent people or animals from coming onto your property, which is why you should never leave your dog unsupervised in an invisibly fenced area. There is some controversy regarding invisible fences, the type of correction they give the dog, and whether that correction is humane. The bottom line, regardless of opinions, is that you must do what you feel is best for your dog.

Invisible fencing lets you restrict your dog's access to certain areas, like swimming pools, driveways, or decorative gardens. For this kind of fencing to be used humanely, your dog must be taught to respect the barrier. Hire a qualified professional dog trainer to help you teach your dog where the boundaries are and how to avoid getting corrected.

Although this book promotes positive training methods, if you can't afford to fence your yard properly, an invisible fence is much better than doing nothing. Not using preventative measures increases the risk that the dog may get lost or killed. Keep in mind that some dogs are not bothered by the electrical correction and will run through it. A physical barrier in the form of chain link or solid wood is a better choice for dogs like these.

Front Door Safety

Making sure your dog doesn't slip out the front door is essential to keeping him safe. Try to prevent front-door escapes by thinking ahead and perhaps denying access to the door through which your dog is most likely to escape. Tighten your screen door so that it closes more quickly, or put a baby gate that locks in the doorway to prevent escapes. Teach your children to be mindful of where the dog is when they are coming and going. Put your dog in a crate or gated room when there are a lot of kids and adults coming and going. Family parties and holiday gatherings are notorious times for dogs to escape and get hit by cars. When you have less control of the home environment, pay special attention to your dog's environment; prevention is half the cure.

FACT

Prevention begins in puppyhood. Start taking your nine- to twelve-week-old puppy to every safe place you can find outdoors and let him off his leash. At this age, most puppies are not confident enough to take off on you and usually stay within range and check in often. Reward each check-in with clicks and treats.

Spend some time teaching your dog appropriate door manners, like sitting and staying without going through the door (even if it's wide open) until told to do so. This requires lots of on-leash setups with a helper to hold the leash in case your dog tries to make a break. You'll want to practice at first with the door shut and then gradually build up to your dog holding the Stay while you open and close the door. You can even increase the difficulty by actually going through the door and leaving the dog in a Stay. The key point to remember here is to reinforce the dog for holding the Stay, not coming through the door. Make sure you practice often and provide a high rate of reinforcement for the right behavior.

Teaching your dog reliable recall is probably a more complicated task than you ever imagined. It is not strictly a training issue but a relationship and management issue as well. Teaching a strong foundation for Come is essential to getting your dog to realize that you are worth paying attention to even in a new environment. Once you have accomplished this reliably, your job will then be to change the variables and get your dog to perform the basic task of looking back at you around all different kinds of distractions. In addition to investing the time it will take to teach your dog a reliable recall, take the steps necessary to create a safe and limited environment that he can enjoy.

CHAPTER 18

Jumping on People

A common behavior problem that dog owners have to deal with is their dogs jumping on people. Sometimes the owner of a jumping maniac may stop having visitors because the jumping is so intense. Jumping is natural for dogs that love to be around people, but your dog must function acceptably both in your home and in public.

Why Do Dogs Jump?

Jumping up on people is one way to get attention. Since dogs do what works, the problem can perpetuate itself to the point where the dog jumps constantly. It is important to understand where jumping comes from and what causes dogs to do this unlikable behavior. Dogs in a pack situation greet each other face to face, and after a few licks and sniffs they decide whether they are friend or foe and proceed to play or fight. When they have been away from their group for a prolonged period of time, they greet each other with a combination of licking and sniffing to re-establish their status within the group and find out where their family members have been.

QUESTION?

What do I do with people who invite my dog to jump?
Being consistent is a very important part of training. Be clear about what the rules are and be a strong advocate for your dog. It is imperative that while you are teaching your dog an alternate behavior, no one—however well meaning—sabotages that plan.

When pet dogs jump on us, they are trying to get to our faces to greet us in a similar manner. This natural behavior, which is actually a gesture of affection and happiness, can easily scare or offend strangers—or owners—resulting in the dog being isolated from the very people she is trying so hard to be with. Dogs that are exuberant greeters need to be taught appropriate manners around guests so that they can be part of family life. After all, jumping works: It gets people to pay attention to them!

The Welcoming Committee

Many people don't like it when their dog jumps on them and place a lot of emphasis on stopping the behavior of jumping. In truth, they are barking up the wrong tree. It is far more effective to define what you prefer the dog to do instead. It is more likely that you will reach your goal if you know what behavior you are looking for so that you can reward your dog for performing the right behavior.

Emphasizing what you want the dog to do by noticing it and rewarding it will help you achieve your goal of a better-mannered pet. Most people choose to have their dogs Sit and Stay when they say hello to people; this is a clear goal for the dog to accomplish and can be used in place of the jumping behavior. You should teach your dog how to Sit and Stay and reinforce it generously when he offers it around people.

ALERT!

Your dog won't learn not to jump right away, so take steps to manage his problem before he masters the correct behavior. This may involve keeping your dog in another room when guests arrive or putting your foot on his leash to prevent him from jumping any time there are people around.

Build a History

Rewarding your dog for the right behavior over and over makes the right behavior a more likely choice when your dog is faced with greeting new people. Dogs do what works; if sitting is rewarded when he greets new people, he will try sitting as his first choice. This is where knowing what you want your dog to do comes in handy. If a Sit/Stay is what you want the dog to do, then you must reinforce it often and handsomely.

The way to change unwanted behavior is to heavily reinforce appropriate behavior and keep your dog from practicing the wrong behavior as much as possible. For instance, when a guest is visiting, keep a leash on your dog so that you can step on it whenever necessary to prevent your dog from jumping. Click and treat the dog anytime she sits without being asked to. Have the guest go away and try again, but this time, ask for Sit only once. If it happens, click and treat; if it doesn't, the guest goes away. The dog learns by trial and error that if he wants the visitor to stay, he must sit; if he doesn't sit, the guest will leave.

This exercise assumes that you have taught your dog to respond to the Sit command and that you have practiced it in all different environments with lots of different types of distractions. Apply the Ten in a Row rule to see if your dog really knows how to Sit in each new environment. Do this by asking your dog to Sit ten times in a row without a click or treat; praise each correct repetition. If he doesn't get ten out of ten correct, you have more training to do. Go back to drilling and practicing with him with this distraction until he can pass the test.

If your dog has only a vague idea of what Sit and Stay mean, it is essential that you review with him in a quiet place with few distractions. You can't expect a dog that can barely Sit and Stay where there are no distractions to Sit and Stay when there are people to jump on.

Provide Lots of Opportunities to Practice

There is nothing like repetition to aid the learning process. The more opportunities the learner has to practice the desirable behavior and get rewarded for it, the more likely the learner is to offer this new behavior in real life. Making, short interesting training sessions—with lots of changes in variables and delicious treats, toys, and games as rewards—will set you on your way to having a dog that knows what to do and does it because you have taught him. Setting up lots of training sessions where you practice different types of greetings will help your dog gain the experience he needs to have good manners anywhere.

Lots of different things are happening when a dog is learning how to greet people without putting his paws on them. Change these variables slowly enough to maintain the dog's response to the command yet with enough variation to challenge him a bit. This is the key to successful training. Every session will take you that much closer to your goal of a well-mannered pet. Some of the training scenarios for teaching or practicing a polite greeting are:

- A person greeting you and your dog while you are out on a walk
- A visitor at the front door
- A person greeting your dog at the pet store, the vet, or the groomer
- A person with a dog greeting you and your dog

- A person sitting somewhere and you and your dog approach them
- A person walking up to you while you are sitting with your dog
- A child greeting your dog
- A person with food greeting your dog

The more combinations of variables you train for, the more reliable your dog will be and the more likely he will be to offer a Sit/Stay behavior instead of jumping. The key to having things run smoothly is to change only one variable at a time. Don't be afraid to go back and review Sit/Stay in places your dog has never been or places where he has a history of jumping and obnoxious behavior. Start off in places where you can get your dog's attention easily, and gradually build up to places that are very distracting for him.

FACT

When trying to get rid of undesirable behavior, you must consistently set your dog up to succeed. Limit his options, give him every chance to get it right, and reward him when he does. Setting your dog up to succeed will help your dog learn what is expected of him and make him a more pleasant companion to have around.

Define Your Dog's Greatest Distraction

Figuring out what makes your dog lose control in different environments will help you break your training sessions down into smaller pieces, making it easier for your dog to be successful. It is important that you do not try to train your dog when she is totally out of control, because she isn't thinking about learning or paying attention. It is a more valuable use of your time to take it slow and add in one distraction at a time until your dog learns to ignore all distractions and stay focused on you instead.

Take a minute to think about where you are likely to meet people when you are out on your walk and try to determine the circumstances around her jumping. Does your dog go crazy when she meets new people while you are out for a walk? Are they passing you on the street or approaching you while you are sitting somewhere? What scenario distracts her the most, and what are the circumstances leading up to it? Some of the distractions that dogs find irresistible are company at your front door, your children coming home from school, your relatives visiting, and meeting people with dogs at the park. Defining the circumstances around which your dog loses control is useful since it gives you an idea of where to start and what you will be working toward.

ALERT!

Just as your dog did not start jumping overnight, she will not suddenly stop. Taking the time to recruit your family and friends as mock guests will allow you to set up training sessions that mimic real life and let your dog learn that she must Sit and Stay in front of people instead of jumping on them.

If your dog is totally out of control around people who come to the door, for instance, you could break the distraction down into smaller pieces. One of your training sessions could start by practicing Sit and Stay in front of the closed door with no guest. Then you could add a family member as the guest, then put the family member outside the door, then add a knock or the doorbell, and eventually build up to being able to practice this with real guests. Breaking the hardest distractions down into small training sessions that introduce one aspect of the distraction at a time is the key for helping your dog learn a new response in a stimulating environment.

If your dog is more of an outdoor kind of jumper that gets overexcited in play and starts mugging you for the ball, using a leash might help you manage this behavior while you reward her for doing something more appropriate instead. When the dog is excited, ask for Sit once. If she sits, click and throw the ball; if not, tell her "too bad" and walk away for a minute or two and try again after a couple of minutes. The click marks the behavior of sitting on the first try, and the dog's reward is the toss of the ball. What better way to teach your dog some self-control than to make the throwing of the ball dependent upon her response to the Sit command. Once she catches on, even a really energetic dog will love this game. Using games is a great way to enrich your relationship with your dog while fine-tuning her response to basic obedience commands and general control issues.

Teaching Sit/Stay with Duration

The duration of a behavior refers to how long the dog has to do the behavior to get reinforced. To avoid jumping, you want the dog to Sit and Stay for an extended period of time. You'll want to extend this period of time slowly until your dog will hold the position without trying to jump for one to two minutes. Eventually you'll also want to have your dog perform the Sit/Stay despite the distractions of people or other dogs.

Although you learned how to shape behavior for Sit/Stay in Chapter 5, take a moment to review it for these circumstances:

1. Use a treat to lure his nose upward and move your hand slightly back.
2. When his bottom hits the floor, click and treat.
3. Repeat this until your dog is offering Sit readily when he sees your hand above his head.
4. Practice without the treat in your hand. Click when his bottom hits the floor and follow up with a treat.
5. Put the treats off your person and repeat, running with the dog to go get the treat after you click for his bottom hitting the ground.
6. Introduce distractions or train somewhere new and go back to the beginning if necessary.
7. Change the variables to mimic the ones that happen in real life: people at the park, on the street, at the pet store, and at home.
8. Build duration in a nondistracting environment and increase it to double the amount of time you'll think you need. To build duration, simply count extra seconds between clicks and treats until your dog is easily waiting twenty to forty seconds for his click and treat.

Building in a long duration for Sit/Stay will help you in public when there are lots of distractions. In practice you may be working on thirty seconds and in real life your dog may give you only fifteen seconds, but it's a start.

Even fifteen seconds will give you time to react quickly enough to keep your dog from putting his paws on a visitor.

Creating a Sitting Maniac

It isn't hard to get a dog hooked on a behavior that works, but it does take time and thought along the way. Jumping is a natural behavior gone astray through inappropriate reinforcement of the wrong behavior. There is nothing difficult about teaching your dog to Sit instead of jump; it just needs to be practiced in increasingly distracting environments until your dog adopts it as second nature. Remember, as with any bad habit, it takes time and patience to change unwanted behavior. Through lots of repetitions and opportunities to practice the right behavior, you will find that your dog will be sitting for attention instead of mugging people. Owning a dog that knows how to greet guests politely makes it easier to take your dog anywhere and have her actively involved in your life.

FACT

The absence of reinforcement for undesirable behavior can be a powerful message. Dogs expect the people they jump on to acknowledge them in some way. Train the people in your family to turn and walk away from your jumping dog without any contact.

Sit for a Treat

One great activity to keep things interesting for puppies is the Sit for a Treat game. To play this game in a group-dog setting, take your dog off her leash and wander around the room greeting other puppies. Approach one of the other puppies with your dog and have the owner of that puppy ask her dog to Sit, asking only once. If the pup sits on the first try, click and treat and move on to the next dog. If the puppy doesn't sit on the first try, simply walk away and ignore the pup, moving on to the next one. Sometimes if the puppies are very high energy it takes awhile for them to catch on, but pretty soon several pups will be sitting perfectly in the middle of the room while the rest are running all willy-nilly around them. One or two lone pups may be sitting stoically, refusing to move for anything. They know exactly what they need to do to get people to pay attention to them.

Play this game at home by inviting a bunch of family or friends over and doing the same exercise. Have everyone wander around, armed with clickers and treats, and take turns giving only one command to Sit and clicking and treating your dog for responding on the first try. Pretty soon, you will see your dog going from person to person, sitting as fast as her rear end will let her to earn her goody.

Changing the Variables

When teaching dogs to sit instead of jump on people in greeting, remember that each variable must be considered and trained for the dog to be reliable. A variable is a circumstance under which we expect the dog to perform the behavior. Some examples of variables for sitting instead of jumping are:

- People are standing in front of the dog indoors.
- People are standing in front of the dog outdoors.
- People are sitting indoors.
- People are sitting outdoors.
- The person being greeted has a dog with them.
- The person being greeted is carrying a box or other item.
- The person being greeted is carrying a child or infant.
- The person being greeted is holding a plate of food.
- The person is walking by the dog and stops to greet her.
- The person is greeting the dog in a very stimulating environment.

The circumstance surrounding each situation must be addressed so that the dog can learn to be successful in all of the different circumstances. Reliability is achieved when the dog understands that no matter what the circumstances—where she is and whom she is greeting—the only behavior that pays off is the sit behavior. Remember that consequences drive behavior. If sitting is the rewardable event, sitting will become a habit around all the people the dog meets.

CHAPTER 19

Dogs That Dig

Does your backyard look like an archaeological dig? Some dogs dig huge craters that resemble dirt swimming pools, while other canine archaeologists prefer to leave dozens of smaller holes that are more conducive to ankle breaking. Regardless of your dog's digging style, most dogs find digging a pleasurable and self-rewarding activity, and once they get going it can be hard to stop them.

19

Why Do Dogs Dig?

Most of the terrier breeds were bred to dig out vermin, mice, rats, and moles. For them, digging is instinctive. Generally, however, dogs dig for a variety of reasons, including boredom, frustration, lack of exercise, and a real need to stay cool on a hot day. Looking at some of the reasons for digging might help you get to the bottom of your dog's problem.

FACT

Mental and physical exercise are both good ways to combat unwanted digging. Anything you add to your dog's day will make him less likely to turn to digging to release his excess energy. Make sure your dog has been properly exercised and has tasks or toys to occupy him.

Bored or Breed?

Digging is a natural behavior among dogs, and most breeds will dig given half the chance. Digging is a wonderful stress reliever, a great way to find a cool spot on a hot day, and for many breeds it is simply in their genetic makeup. Many of the terriers, bred to hunt up vermin, will dig for voles or other creatures, making the backyard look like a minefield. Huskies, German shepherds, golden retrievers, beagles, and other breeds dig for the fun of it. Being able to determine the motive for your dog's digging may give you some insight into what you can do to redirect him to a less damaging hobby. A dog that is bored can be distracted by more exercise and something to chew on. A dog that has an innate desire to dig can be given a sandbox or other type of digging pit to satisfy his need to dig. Dogs with other motives might need sheer supervision so that inappropriate digging can be redirected elsewhere or discouraged outright. If boredom is the reason for digging, you can buy many different kinds of toys to help. But remember, too much time alone is not good for a dog and will lead to behavior problems no matter how much stimulation and how many toys you provide. There is nothing quite like your undivided attention!

Bored dogs cause destruction. A dog with nothing to do will bark, howl, chew, destroy, and dig. Digging is a great stress reliever, and digging up whatever treasures a dog can find is well worth the effort. If you think that boredom may be your dog's motive for digging, take steps to improve his environment now. Provide lots of safe, interesting toys, and rotate them regularly. Take your dog for a romp in the woods, play with other dogs at the park, or teach him tricks. Invite a friend's dog to spend the afternoon playing and wrestling with your dog. Mental exercise also gives him something rewarding to do besides digging. Try the following workouts:

- Stuff Kong toys with dog food and peanut butter and let your dog figure out how to get the food out. Freeze the toy to make this an even cooler challenge on a hot day.
- Buy interesting toys for your dog and rotate them weekly so that your dog always has something new to play with.
- Put treats in all different places in the yard for your dog to find.
- Put your dog's meals in a treat-dispensing toy and let him work for his dinner.
- Put peanut butter or cream cheese on the inside of the shaft of an uncooked marrow bone. Your dog will have a blast licking it out.
- Make some agility equipment—tunnels, ramps, and jumps—and teach your dog to negotiate them with and without your help.

Remember that dogs need a variety of play, training, and exercise to be happy, healthy, and content family pets. When any behavior is extreme, like digging or barking, it usually is an advertisement for needing more of something. In most cases, it's that the dog is bored and frustrated because he does not get enough exercise or one-on-one time with his owner.

FACT

Playtime with other dogs is a great stress buster and an essential part of the day for the average active dog. Invite a dog friend over on a regular basis to help you tire out your active dog, or consider enrolling your pooch in a well-run doggie day care.

Frustration

If your dog is unsupervised in a fenced yard or dog pen, he may start to dig out of frustration. Your dog can see and hear people passing by, but he can't get to where the action is. A dog that is frustrated by being confined for too long will often try to dig his way to freedom. Don't leave your dog unattended for long periods of time, and stimulate his environment by hiding toys packed with his dinner and treats or hiding bones and things to chew in the area where he is confined. Go out and play with him and distract him from digging if he does it while you are present.

If your dog tries to dig out of the yard, you may want to bury ¼-inch mesh wire along the fence line to make it impossible to dig past a certain depth. Most dogs get discouraged and find other pursuits once they hit something that won't let them dig any deeper. The best way to alleviate frustration is to spend more time with your dog and provide him with more things to think about.

Exercise

If there is one thing that can save you time in the long run, it's providing your dog with enough exercise. The more opportunities your dog gets to run, chase, swim, wrestle, roll, and romp, the less energy he will have to dig holes. If you own an active dog—and most diggers are very active—he will need at least one to three hours of exercise daily. Whether you take him for long runs in the woods, allow him off-leash time to play with other dogs, or enroll him in a doggie day care program, he needs his exercise. Make sure you're doing what you can to meet his basic needs before you complain about the digging.

ALERT!

If you have a digger, it is vital to check the perimeter of your fence periodically for holes through which your dog can escape. Block holes near the perimeter of the fence is with ¼-inch mesh wire buried in the hole and covered with crushed stone or a ¾-inch layer of rocks and soil.

Prevention is Key

The best way to stop digging is to prevent it in the first place. Diggers are greatly reinforced by the activity of digging. It's great fun to dig a huge hole in the ground and plop down in it and inhale all the delicious smells. Digging will be a hard habit to break without the proper redirection and supervision from you.

First Steps

Preventing digging in puppyhood by not leaving your puppy unattended in the yard is a key ingredient in training a puppy to grow up entertaining herself in other ways. If you are there when your puppy first tries to dig and you can effectively redirect it, bad habits won't get started, and you'll reap the rewards of a nice hole-free yard. Distractions can take the form of toys, games, or showing your puppy where she can dig. This input from you is critical for helping your dog learn the rules of the yard. If you aren't there, you can't teach her!

Provide Shade

Not paying attention to a dog's basic need to be cool on a hot day may contribute to your dog's digging problem. On a hot day, a dog's instincts tell her to find a cool, dry place to rest. In the absence of adequate shade, she will often dig a hole and lie in it. Digging a hole to lie in is a natural way for the dog to cool herself on a hot day. If your dog is outdoors in hot weather, provide plenty of shade, shelter, and water, or consider leaving her indoors with the air conditioning on or a fan running. All dogs have a different sensitivity to heat and cold; observe your dog for signs that it's too hot or too cold for her outdoors. Here are some ideas for keeping cool on a hot day:

- Set up a beach umbrella and a kiddie wading pool in the yard.
- Put some ice cubes in your dog's water bowl.
- Freeze some dog biscuits in water and put them in the wading pool.
- Get a special sun-reflecting tarp and secure it over your dog's outdoor pen.

For the sake of his comfort—and health—you need to provide your dog with plenty of water and shade on hot days. Make sure that even an active pooch is not allowed to overdo it with play and exercise. Try taking your dog out for exercise early in the morning or after the sun goes down to prevent heat stroke.

Legal Digging Zone

Dogs whose genetics tell them to dig need alternative outlets for their enthusiastic escapades. Replacing the inappropriate behavior with a more appropriate one is the only permanent solution. If digging comes naturally to these dogs, why not provide a safe, legal place for them to dig by making a digging pit? A digging pit can be any size, but 4" × 4" for small dogs and 8" × 8" for larger breeds can be a general guideline. Use garden timbers to make a box shape and fill the box with sand. You may actually want to dig out the existing soil and make a bed of stone for the bottom to supply good drainage. This way, regardless of the climate, it won't become a mud puddle in inclement weather. Fill the rest of the pit with play sand, the kind used in children's sandboxes. Use a metal rake to evenly distribute the sand.

You may want to invest in a metal rake so that you can clear any uncovered treasure from the digging pit and keep the sand loose and inviting. You may also want to add fresh sand periodically to provide plenty of places to hide new goodies.

Now comes the fun part! Bury toys, bones, rawhide, dog cookies, balls, and other surprises for your dog to find. Make some of the treasures easy to find, others more difficult. The more of a digger your dog is, the more challenging you should make the treasure hunt. Periodically (once a week) you should hide new treasures and rake the pit to remove any old cookies, bones, or other treats. If you are creative in what you bury, your active dog will know exactly where to dig to find the good stuff. Here are some ideas for buried treasure:

- Hard dog cookies
- Kongs stuffed with peanut butter and treats
- Marrow bones (Buy ones from the butcher; uncooked is safest.)
- Rawhide sticks, bones, and chips
- Pig ears smeared with cream cheese inside a paper bag
- A small cardboard jewelry box filled with treats
- A cardboard ice-cream box with treats or a chew toy inside
- A favorite toy, like a ball or a stuffed animal, in a paper bag

Regardless of the treasure, be sure it is something that your dog can safely have unattended. Experiment while you are watching him to be sure he doesn't eat anything that he shouldn't (like the paper that you've hidden the tennis ball in). A certain amount of shredding is fine; you just don't want him eating the entire empty ice-cream container.

QUESTION?

How do you fill in existing holes?
There are many theories about what to do about the holes that your dog has already dug. Some people leave the holes alone and the dog only digs in the holes he's made. Other people put large rocks in the existing holes before filling them in. Experiment to see what works best for your dog.

Two solutions for digging that work for some folks are to bury some of the dog's feces in each hole, or bury ¼-inch mesh wire about one to two inches under the soil. In the first case, the dog uncovers something she thinks she's buried before. In the latter, when she hits the mesh, she can't go any deeper and gives up.

Regardless of what you try as a solution to stop your canine archaeologist from turning your yard into the Grand Canyon, the only way to really stop a digger is not to give him the opportunity to dig in inappropriate places. Supervise him closely, don't leave him unattended in the yard, and consider building him a digging area of his own. A dog that really enjoys digging will love the opportunity to practice it legally. You'll notice that there are no suggestions here regarding punishment. Excessive digging is a symptom of a larger problem. Digging is the dog's way of releasing pent-up energy, boredom, and frustration. Alleviate your dog's boredom by signing him up for fun obedience classes or by taking a class to teach your dog tricks or agility, and be sure to regularly provide stimulating toys that he doesn't see every day. If you are creative in providing lots of stimulating activities for your dog, you will be rewarded with a calm, more content family pet and a lot fewer holes in your backyard.

CHAPTER 20

Canine Social Skills

Dogs are social animals that learn to interact and get along with each other by playing together from a very young age. The best way for them to learn how to get along is for them to play with lots of other dogs during the most impressionable time in their lives—the first eight to eighteen weeks of age.

Socialization Versus Training

Training a dog the basics of Sit, Stay, and Come can be accomplished at any age, but the ideal time to socialize your dog to other dogs, people, and new experiences is between the ages of eight and eighteen weeks. Once a puppy reaches eighteen weeks, she is less open to new experiences, and she begins to gravitate toward the familiar rather than explore the new. You must of course continue to give your dog social experiences beyond the age of eighteen weeks, but if you don't start before then you are sentencing your dog to a life of fearful and suspicious reactions to other dogs, new experiences, and people.

What Is Socialization?

Socializing a dog is an investment of time and energy. It should include experiences with other dogs, interactions with people of all shapes and sizes, and exposure to brand new environments. It isn't good enough to just show up in public; careful planning is required to make sure your dog has positive experiences that will benefit her for a lifetime. Giving your dog a varied experience of life will teach her from an early age to cope with sounds, sights, smells, new people, and a variety of breeds and mixed breeds of dogs. By making an effort to socialize your dog, you are increasing your dog's ability to learn how to act around people and other dogs, and you are giving her the best chance of becoming a well-mannered and friendly adult dog. A good solid social experience will benefit her for a lifetime.

Although it's imperative to begin socialization around the first month of a puppy's life, it's also important to keep at it so the dog remains open to new experiences. A dog that consistently encounters new things, places, and people will remain well socialized.

Dogs have a critical socialization window during which they should meet at least a hundred people and a hundred other dogs and puppies.

The window opens around the second week of life when the puppies first open their eyes, and the window starts to close around the eighteenth week. This doesn't mean that socialization stops there. It must continue beyond this point, but it means that your puppy is most impressionable at this age and can accept new experiences more easily than an older dog. The more positive experiences your puppy has during this time with people and other dogs, the more willing she will be to accept and get along with people and dogs for the rest of her life. You can make or break a dog's potential by offering the right socialization at the right time.

ALERT!

Socialization is not the same for every dog. There are as many personality types among dogs as there are among people: Some are outgoing, some are shy, some are overbearing, some are vocal, some are physical, and so on. A puppy's play style will often determine what types of puppies she should play with to learn the right ways to get along with other dogs.

Don't Wait!

Don't wait until your dog is fully vaccinated to begin socializing her, but do carefully choose the dogs she meets and plays with. It isn't a good idea to take a pup that is between eight and twelve weeks old to the local park and let her meet just any old dog or eat other dogs' feces. Enroll your young dog in a well-organized puppy kindergarten class before she is sixteen weeks old and make sure that all the puppies attending the class have been started on their vaccinations.

Most puppies get their last series of shots at sixteen weeks of age, but if you wait until your dog is that old to get her around other dogs, you will probably find that she is shy and defensive and not as outgoing and adventurous as she may have been at an earlier age. This is a sign that the socialization window is closing, and you need to increase and intensify her experience around other dogs. In short, if you wait to begin your dog's socialization until she is fully vaccinated, you will find you have to work harder at getting her to like being around other dogs. More dogs die every year from behavior problems that stem from a lack of socialization than dogs exposed to the diseases we vaccinate against. So get out there and make sure every puppy you ever own gets to meet lots of other dogs and people so she avoids becoming another statistic.

FACT

A varied social experience is an insurance policy against bad experiences that might alter a dog's future behavior. Because they will have a lot of experience to draw upon, they will be able to go back to enjoying the experience of being with other dogs.

Socializing Your Dog to Other Dogs

Socialization to other dogs is perhaps the most overlooked aspect of a dog's social experience. The more dogs and puppies a young dog meets, the better he will get along with any dog, anywhere. Not supplying your dog with the skills with which to get along with other dogs may well be a form of abuse and neglect. When a dog has enough social experience with other dogs during his critical window of socialization, he learns how to get along with dogs. Without the right kind of social experience, behavior problems develop. Most owners who seek private training for their aggressive dogs have dogs who were not socialized properly and never learned their valuable social skills.

Pay Attention to Play Styles

Rowdy puppies should not be allowed to play rough for long periods of time. By having active dogs play with other dogs of varying personality types—shy puppies, outgoing adolescents, and adult dogs (who are not as tolerant of rude puppy antics)—you have the best chance of teaching the boisterous puppy how to adjust his play style to any dog. Letting a rowdy puppy play only with other rowdy puppies is asking for trouble. This pup will grow up to be obnoxious around other dogs and will not be well liked. Obnoxious adult dogs are not tolerated well by other adult dogs because they have no manners. They jump, roughhouse, and mouth too roughly. As a result, they are often overcorrected by other dogs. The rowdy adult dog is often the dog that all the other dogs gang up on because all the other dogs feel he needs to be taught a lesson. The rowdy pup needs lots of social experience. Consider doggie day care to help him meet all kinds of dogs that will teach him the rules of getting along with the group.

To preserve your dog's healthy social development, monitor his playmates so that he's not playing too rough for too long a period of time. Some rough play is okay, but too much will teach your puppy that being out of control is the way to play. Vary your dog's experience by going new places and meeting lots of different dogs.

Playful puppies are middle-of-the-road types; they can play rough with the rowdy dog or tone it down to play with the shyer dogs. They are born peacemakers and party dogs. These pups can be with any type of dog and have a great experience. These cheerleaders will invite any dog to play and will be the most easygoing dog in the group. Owners of this type of pup need to be careful that their puppies don't get too overwhelmed by more enthusiastic dogs. Don't be afraid to initiate little breaks in the action and let your dog cool down a bit before sending her back in for more fun.

Unlike rowdy or energetic pups, shy dogs would wilt in a group of rowdy pups, learning to be fearful and defensive instead of playful. These dogs should spend huge amounts of time with playful pups that invite them to play but are not too boisterous. Playful puppies invite shy dogs to interact by play bowing, barking (not excessively), and kissing the other puppies. The playful puppy will continue to invite the shy pup to play until eventually he wears him down. A shy puppy needs triple the amount of social experience as the average dog, but it needs to be carefully calculated so as not to overwhelm him. If you own a shy puppy, enroll him in a well-organized puppy kindergarten and consider a carefully selected dog-gie day care. Be sure the day care folks know how to socialize a shy dog and provide downtime via a nap in a crate or separate room several times throughout the day.

Socialization to People

The easiest part of socializing a puppy simply involves showing up in public with a clicker and treats to make sure all new experiences are fun and rewarding. Bring plenty of delicious treats and a toy to keep the puppy's mouthing under control. Go to parks and pet stores, or visit the groomer or the neighbors. Take your puppy to as many new places as possible; let her hear, see, and experience the world. Be careful how you introduce your puppy to these new experiences, though. If she seems afraid or unsure of herself, go slowly. Try backing off a bit, using your best treats and happy voice to encourage your puppy to investigate.

ALERT!

Never force an unwilling puppy to investigate something she's terrified of; a bad experience can set you back weeks. Building confidence is a slow process, which works best if you provide your puppy with proof that the world is a safe and interesting place.

When a puppy is fearful of new people and strange things, the best way to help build her confidence is to let her take his time warming up and reward her bravery. A dog can't learn anything when she is afraid—so don't force her. By working at your dog's comfort level you are putting money in the bank for building confidence. Keep the experience fun, upbeat, and varied, and your puppy will develop into a confident adult dog.

Start Early

The more early interaction you can provide, the easier it will be for your pup to learn to cope with new experiences. By having some tricks up your sleeve, you will have more options in helping your puppy to have good experiences regardless of the circumstances.

1. Teach your pup how to target your hand (see Chapter 4) and use this to introduce new people and objects.
2. Work at your pup's comfort level with the goal being to gradually get her closer.
3. Go to at least two new places each week.
4. Continue to help your dog have good experiences despite the extra effort.
5. Get out there. There is harm in waiting.
6. Continue past eighteen weeks of age, but start sooner than four weeks if possible.
7. Enlist the help of family and friends.
8. Break scary new experiences into small attainable goals.
9. Avoid moving too fast; if you overwhelm your pup, don't be afraid to quit and try again later.

Some Dogs Need More Social Experience

Depending on your dog's breed and personality, she may need more social experience than average. The working and herding breeds are notoriously more suspicious of new people and experiences. If you think about what these dogs do for work, it makes a lot of sense. Working and herding dogs are bred to notice and react to what is foreign, which is what makes them so good at herding and guarding. No wonder they need double the amount of socialization than the average dog. Socialization conditions them not to overreact when they encounter something unfamiliar. The more good experiences they have, the better able they will be to accept new people and things as a normal part of their world.

What about Doggie Day Care?

Doggie day care facilities are popping up all over the place to provide dogs with nonstop canine fun. Active dogs enjoy wrestling and playing with other dogs, and they get lots of attention from the human staff. Day care a few times a week or every day can make a huge difference in the hours you spend together at home and on the weekends. Most working people come home too tired to exercise an active dog for two hours. With doggie day care, however, that same owner could spend those two hours enjoying life with her dog in some other way.

Day care is a great way to give an active dog an outlet for all his energy, a shy dog an opportunity for new experiences, and a boisterous dog a chance to meet all kinds of dogs. It can help all types of dogs learn how to adjust their play style to be more compatible with their playmates. The following are some tips for identifying the right doggie day care:

- The dogs should have their own water bowls to prevent the spread of viruses.
- The dogs should be separated into groups according to age, personality, and play style, with no more than ten to fifteen dogs per group.
- An enhanced rest time via crates, separate mats, or runs should be part of the day. This ensures that active dogs learn self-control and shy or playful ones get a break from the other dogs.
- There should be one attendant for every ten dogs.
- Day care attendants should be adults who have been properly trained in normal (and abnormal) dog behavior, including how to safely break up a dogfight.
- A strong disinfectant and anti-viral solution should be used to clean up accidents.
- All dogs should be required to be vaccinated or titered and spayed or neutered.
- All dogs should be in good health and not have symptoms of vomiting, diarrhea, eye discharge, or coughing.
- Dogs that are aggressive toward people or other dogs should not be allowed at day care for the safety of everyone.
- Go in person to meet the staff and see how they run their day and make sure the indoor and outdoor facilities are clean and secure.

The best candidates for day care are puppies and young adult dogs. If you are unable to get your dog out to lots of different places to play with other dogs, day care may be a great option for you.

Most doggie day care facilities will interview you and your dog, which gives you the opportunity to see the facility and ask questions. Go with a checklist and be sure you are comfortable with the style of the day care facility before leaving your dog there. Interview at several places and talk to other dog owners before you make your decision.

QUESTION?

What is a vaccine titer?
A vaccine titer is a blood test performed on a vaccinated dog to determine his level of immunity to a given disease. In general, if a titer is positive, the animal has immunity to that particular disease. If the animal does not have a positive titer, consult your veterinarian before having your pet revaccinated.

Abused or Unsocialized?

Many dog owners mistakenly assume that their adopted or rescued dog was abused because they are shy or aggressive around new people or dogs. These dogs tend to cower and shake or act aggressive. The reality is often that the dog has not been socialized to people, dogs, and new experiences, and she reacts aggressively or shyly out of fear and lack of confidence.

Aggression and Fear in Unsocialized Dogs

Lack of early socialization is usually the reason for fear and aggression issues later in life. If a dog does not experience the world while she is young and associate her experiences with good things, there will be problems later in life. Sometimes, these will be too complicated to fix completely. It's hard to manage a dog that doesn't like children, is aggressive to other dogs, and is afraid of the car. All of these problems are preventable if a puppy gets enough exposure to life. If you are raising a puppy, make sure she meets and plays with at least 100 other dogs and puppies, 100 people—especially men and children—and visits at least 100 different places before she turns five months old. This is the most predictive way to prevent aggression and fears and the way to raise the most stable dog possible. If yours is a shelter or rescued dog, you can't turn back the clock, but you can do a lot to make sure that each new experience is a good one and build from there. If your rescued dog is a damaged one, learning the skills you need to help her work through her fears and aggression and learn to become a polite member of society is your commitment to her.

Helping Unsocialized Dogs

The best way to help a dog that behaves in this manner is to train her and build her confidence around new people, dogs, and experiences. Making excuses for shy or aggressive dogs or trying to cuddle and comfort them will not fix the problem, and it could make it worse. Remedial socialization (socializing a dog after the optimum age of eight to eighteen weeks) is time consuming and fraught with regression and frustration, but ultimately it is well worth the effort. Some socialization tips for shy or aggressive dogs include:

1. Teach your dog how to target your hand and extend it to people and objects.
2. Build confidence slowly by taking your time and allowing for regression.
3. Increase the distance by backing away from the person or object until the dog is comfortable.
4. If you are working with new people, have them be as neutral as possible. Have them turn to the side, make no direct eye contact with the dog, and let it be the dog's idea to go to them.
5. Use the best treats; you want to associate new experiences with the things the dog really likes.

Be patient and expect setbacks with your unsocialized dog. With time, your dog will become more confident.

CHAPTER 21

Family Dynamics: Problems and Solutions

Adding a dog to your family or starting a family when you have already raised a dog is a unique and challenging time in family life. Whether the process is a smooth one largely depends upon the tools available to you and how well you use them. Each family situation is a little different. The bottom line is each situation can be successful if the family has the right tools to help them.

When Baby Makes Four

The key to a successful introduction is to go slow. The pet you are adopting or the baby you are bringing home to meet the existing dog is going to be with you for a very long time. You don't need to have everyone be best friends immediately. In fact, the less you push for harmony, the less likely it will be to elude you. Harmony comes from a slow, organized, and orchestrated introduction that involves giving each party space and time to get to know one another.

Human siblings need to be prepared for the arrival of a new family member, and dogs are no different. If you are bringing home a new baby from the hospital, bring home a blanket that has the baby's scent on it to give the dog a heads up that a new member of the family will be joining you soon. Recognizing the scent mixed with your scent will often help the dog adjust to the new member of the pack with less anxiety and stress.

How much training and socialization the dog has had and how much exercise he gets after the baby comes all contribute to the family's adjustment once the baby comes home. Here are some tips for helping your dog accept your new baby as a pack member:

- Provide lots of exercise for the dog during the first several months. Hire someone to walk or play with your dog or enlist the services of a reputable doggie day care.
- Pay attention to the schedule. If you don't have one, put a flexible schedule in place before the baby comes.
- Work on greeting people without jumping (teach Sit/Stay instead) before you have the baby so that your dog can be part of the visiting company.
- Teach your dog to like being alone in his crate or in a separate room so you have options during stressful times.
- Never leave a dog alone with a baby even if the baby is strapped into a carrier or other baby minder. Accidents happen. Dogs are curious, and babies make very strange and often scary noises that need to be investigated.
- Teach your dog to walk with a stroller so that he can accompany you on your walks around the neighborhood.

- Set up the nursery and put together all the baby equipment long before the baby comes home. This will help the dog adjust to all the new stuff before the baby comes.
- Keep some delicious treats in a container near where you change and feed the baby. Before you start to feed or change, give one to the dog so he begins to associate your giving your full attention to the baby as a good thing.
- Use your crate, gates, and pens. Lots of dogs, even older ones, deal with stress by chewing their way through the house.

If you are concerned that your dog will have trouble adjusting, you may want to consult a professional dog trainer.

Adding a Dog or Puppy to Your Growing Family

There is nothing more exciting than adding a new furry member to a family. It's many parents' dream to have their kids grow up with a dog to love and care for. How well this goes depends on a couple of things. Do your research before you decide on a breed or mix of breeds. Find out what the dog's exercise requirement is and how much training will be needed to have a calm, relaxed family pet. Look at your own schedule and determine if you are ready for another baby. The process of teaching a dog or puppy to be a well-behaved member of your family is time consuming. Training, socializing, and exercising your new dog can feel like a full-time job, but it is necessary if you want a dog that can be with your children without incident. Dogs don't come knowing how to act around children. They need to be educated and trained so that they behave in ways that are pleasurable and safe for all parties involved. Choosing the right breeder, shelter, or rescue is the key to having a smooth transition. Here are some tips for a rewarding experience:

- Sign your new puppy or adult dog up for a well-run class right away.
- Plan to continue to take classes all during that first year to make sure that yours is the dog that always comes when called and walks on a leash nicely and doesn't jump on every person she meets.

- Plan family activities around socializing the dog. Plan to take your new dog to lots of new places—parks, hikes, pet stores, downtown areas, other peoples houses, dog parks, beaches, soccer games, and school pick ups.

- Assign family members jobs so that the burden of work is spread out and everyone gets to enjoy the fun of owning the dog.

- Make sure your family schedule has cleared for at least six months to raise the puppy or help the adult dog adjust. Have kids cut back on regular sports or activities and make dog training and socialization one of their activities for this period of time.

- Plan ahead and don't allow your new dog or puppy freedom to practice unacceptable behavior. For instance, if she jumps at and bites the kids' friends when they are playing outside, keep her in or supervise her until you have trained her how to behave with kids.

- Plan to use a crate to help housetrain and confine your puppy and adolescent dog until she learns the rules of the house.

- Use your crate on a schedule so that your puppy has rest time and play time in a scheduled pattern throughout the day.

Kid-Proofing Your Pooch

The best way to kid-proof your new dog or puppy is to make sure she gets enough basic socialization. Ideally, you'll want the puppy to meet and play with 100 people and other dogs in as many different places as you can think of. The more good experiences the dog has, the better able she will be to cope with the stress of new, overstimulating, and exciting circumstances of family life. Attending a well-run puppy kindergarten or adult training class will also introduce you to tools you can use to help teach your dog that being handled is a good thing. Building up tolerance for rough handling is a must have for any dog that will live with children. Poking, prodding, hugging, being dragged by the collar, being sat on or ridden, having a child's face close to theirs, loud noises, loud voices, running, bouncing, and jumping are not a dog's favorite activities, but they are a daily reality when they live with kids. Having skills to cope with this is essential. Giving your dog a good association with being handled and the normal rhythms of family life will pay off in years to come.

The joy of owning dogs is an enormous payoff for the amount of work involved in raising them. They are a lot of work, especially initially, when it is so critical that they are properly socialized. The benefit of having a dog that can play with your children, be dressed up for Halloween, attend tea parties and campouts, and go on vacations is well worth the effort of the first year. Remember that the time you spend now is a forward investment. You will reap the benefits of this great new family member for years to come!

Older Dog

Depending on your dog's circumstances, you could be one of several new places she's been lately. You are just another change of scenery for her at first, and it will take some time for her to warm up to you and trust you. You may think you're giving her the greatest home ever, but she may still be mourning a past caregiver or finally feeling used to her most recent situation. Whatever your dog's past holds, she is leaving everything she knows to come to your home, and just as you would respect that change for a puppy, you need to appreciate it when it comes to your new, older dog.

ALERT!

Many adult dogs that are adopted through rescues and shelters were given up for existing behavior problems. Jumping, barking, or pulling on leash may be easy to fix, but aggression toward other dogs or children and separation anxiety are much more serious. Get as much detail as you can from your rescue group, and choose a group that does a considerable amount of temperament evaluation and testing.

The loving attention your older dog needs is similar to that of a new puppy. Be gentle with her, allow her to explore under your watchful supervision, don't pester her, and don't overwhelm her.

Training for Peaceful Co-existence

Training is an important part of raising any puppy or introducing an adult dog to any home, but it is crucial for families who have children or are adding children to their existing dog family. The more training a dog has had, the easier it is to direct him and the smoother the transition to family life with kids will be. Here are some behaviors that are essential in managing your new dog or puppy around your family life:

- **Leave it.** This behavior means stop what you are doing or thinking about doing immediately. This comes in handy for dropped toys, food, or other treasure that the dog thinks are free game.
- **Down/Stay.** If a dog can hold a down and stay there until you have finished your business, you will all keep your sanity.
- **Sit/Stay.** This is the behavior that will replace the wild greeting your dog wants to give every person and other dog he meets. Being able to sit and stay will mean that you will enjoy his company and the kids can have friends visit without being wrestled to the ground in a tangled heap.
- **Walk nicely without pulling.** Otherwise known as heeling, this behavior will allow you to take your dog more places. Having a dog that walks next to you nicely is so much safer and much more pleasant than a dog that pulls you through the streets on a mission that only he knows about.
- **Come when called.** Being able to call your dog to come when he is in the yard or running loose in the woods or park is essential to being able to allow this privilege in the first place. Giving this freedom is wonderful exercise and mental stimulation for dogs, but the dog must be reliable about coming back or it is not an option.

In general, the more you train your dog to comply with these basic behaviors, the better able you will be to offer him privileges and the more fun it will be to take him places and do things together. The point of getting a dog in the first place was so that he could spend time with you doing the things that families do, so make sure he has the skills and knowledge to hold up his end of the bargain and be a polite, pleasant member of your family.

Management Basics

The more structure and house rules you have in the beginning, the more peaceful the homecoming will be. Chaotic households with lots of noise are not a great way to convince a new dog or puppy that she has hit the jackpot and got the best family on the block. Dogs like order and a schedule and thrive in environments that are organized and make sense. They need to be fed and walked on a schedule, they need predictable potty breaks and play time, and they need frequent downtime and naps. Many behavior problems can arise without downtime in a crate for puppies and adolescent dogs or in a gated area for older dogs.

Nap Time

Downtime lets a dog know that it's time to rest, and when this is offered on a regular basis there is a lot less inappropriate behavior, including nipping, mouthing, jumping, and destructive behavior. Out–of-control behavior can be curbed by making sure that your new dog is getting enough downtime. Most dogs will not seek out a bed or crate for a nap when they are puppies or adolescents. Much like children, they can't stand to miss anything despite the fact they are so tired they can barely stand up. Having a safe place to take a nap or chew on a bone is essential for dogs so that they can recharge and have a full rest.

Puppy-Proofing

Limit the amount of space your puppy has to run around—especially when you're not home. Many people confine the pup to a room or group of manageable rooms in the beginning. Choose a room in which there's a lot of people traffic so your puppy doesn't feel isolated. Pick a room that's fairly easy to clean, with an easily washable floor surface. Put up baby gates to keep the puppy in her area. Once your puppy understands what's expected of her with regard to housetraining in her designated area, you can expand the area she's allowed in, still using the baby gates to keep her from rooms that are off limits.

A Word on Crates

If you have a puppy and you've bought a crate that will fit her when she is full grown, she is going to have a lot of room in it. This is not good because she will be able to eat and sleep in one end and eliminate in the other, which defeats all your housetraining efforts. To reduce the amount of room your pup has in the crate, create a divider to put in it so that the space is cut down to about half. As your puppy grows, you can move the divider until she doesn't need it anymore. You can use anything from stiff cardboard to plywood as a divider. Just make sure it's securely positioned so your puppy can't grab an end to chew on and devour it.

Supervision

If there is one thing that families do wrong in trying to introduce a dog into their lives, it is not supervising the children enough so that they are behaving appropriately around the dog. Here is a list of things children need to learn about dogs:

- Children should not take away food, toys, or stolen objects from dogs. This is a job for parents only.
- Children should pet the dog on the neck in a stroking or gentle scratching motion instead of banging on his head.
- Most dogs do not like to be hugged by children or have the child put his face in her face. You can teach your dog to tolerate this, but parents should be cautious with shelter or rescue dogs where not a lot is known about their history.
- Growling means go away. A child should stop what he is doing and tell a parent, who will need to seek the advice and help of a professional to make sure growling doesn't escalate to biting.
- Children should not run around a new dog until the dog has learned to keep its mouth to itself.
- Visiting children need to be taught the rules, and a parent needs to supervise to make sure they are adhered to.

- Children should not interrupt a dog while he is eating. Parents can teach the dog to accept the presence of children while he is eating, but this should always be supervised.
- Children should not jump on or startle a sleeping dog. Parents can teach the child how to call or clap so that the dog wakes up and comes to them.
- Children need to be supervised with new puppies and dogs so that all parties can learn the appropriate way to interact with one another.
- Children should attend training classes with their families to learn how to interact appropriately with their new dog. Older children can participate in training the dog.

The more vigilant a parent is in observing the new dog and the children together, the more successful she will be in redirecting inappropriate behavior and preventing bad habits and undesirable behavior problems from developing. You can't teach anything if you aren't there, and the time you will save not having to fix all the things that have gone wrong will benefit you for years to come.

APPENDIX

Resources

Books

Abrantes, Roger. *Dog Language: An Encyclopedia of Canine Behavior* (Wakan Tanka Publishers, 1997).

Benjamin, Carol. *Dog Problems* (Hungry Minds, Inc., 1989).

Burch, Mary R., and Jon S. Bailey. *How Dogs Learn* (Hungry Minds, Inc., 1999).

Campbell, William E. *Owner's Guide to Better Behavior in Dogs* (Alpine Publishers, 1989).

Campbell, William E. *Behavior Problems in Dogs*, Third Revised Edition (BehaviorRx Systems, 1999).

Cantrell, Krista. *Catch Your Dog Doing Something Right: How to Train Any Dog in Five Minutes a Day* (Plume Publishers, 1998).

Donaldson, Jean. *The Culture Clash* (James and Kenneth Publishing, 1997).

Donaldson, Jean. *Dogs Are from Neptune* (Lasar Multimedia Productions, 1998).

Dunbar, Ian. *Dr. Dunbar's Good Little Dog Book* (James and Kenneth Publishing, 1992).

Dunbar, Ian. *How to Teach a New Dog Old Tricks* (James and Kenneth Publishing, 1998).

Evans, Job Michael. *Training and Explaining: How to Be the Dog Trainer You Want to Be* (Hungry Minds, Inc., 1995).

Fox, Dr. Michael W. *Understanding Your Dog* (St. Martin's Press, 1972).

Milani, D.V.M., Myrna. *The Body Language and Emotions of Dogs* (William Morrow and Company, 1986).

Milani, D.V.M., Myrna. *DogSmart* (Contemporary Publishing, 1997).

Owens, Paul. *The Dog Whisperer: A Compassionate, Nonviolent Approach to Dog Training* (Adams Media Corporation, 1999).

Pryor, Karen. *Don't Shoot the Dog: The New Art of Teaching and Training*, Revised Edition (Bantam Books, 1999).

Reid, Ph.D., Pamela. *Excel-Erated Learning: Explaining in Plain English How Dogs Learn and How Best to Teach Them* (James and Kenneth Publishers, 1996).

Rugaas, Turid. *On Talking Terms with Dogs: Calming Signals* (Legacy By Mail, 1997).

Ryan, Terry. *The Toolbox for Remodeling Your Problem Dog* (Howell Book House, 1998).

Schwartz, Charlotte. *The Howell Book of Puppy Raising* (Hungry Minds, Inc., 1987).

Scott, John Paul and John L. Fuller. *Genetics and the Social Behavior of the Dog* (University of Chicago Press, 1965).

Tellington-Jones, Linda. *Getting in Touch with Your Dog: A Gentle Approach to Influencing Health, Behavior, and Performance* (Trafalgar Square, 2001).

Wilkes, Gary. *A Behavior Sampler* (Sunshine Books, 1994).

Videos

Broitman, Virginia. *Bow Wow, Take 2* (Canine Training Systems, 1996).

Broitman, Virginia and Sherry Lippman. *Take a Bow Wow* (Canine Training Systems, 1996).

Jones, Deborah. *Click & Fetch* (Canine Training Systems, 1999).

Pryor, Karen. *Clicker Magic! The Art of Clicker Training* (Sunshine Books, 1997).

Pryor, Karen. *Puppy Love* (Sunshine Books, 1999).

Rugaas, Turid. *Calming Signals: What Your Dog Tells You* (Legacy By Mail, 2001).

Wilkes, Gary. *Click! & Treat Training Kit* (Click! & Treat Products, 1996).

Wilkes, Gary. *The Doggie Repair Kit* (Click! & Treat Products, 1996).

Organizations

The Association of Pet Dog Trainers (APDT)
800-738-3647
www.apdt.com
Search the database for a list of trainers in your area.

Delta Society
425-226-7357
www.deltasociety.org
E-mail: *info@deltasociety.org*
Information on service dogs

Therapy Dogs International
973-252-9800
www.tdi-dog.org
E-mail: *tdi@gti.net*
Information on therapy dogs

Whole-Dog-Journal.com
800-829-9165
www.whole-dog-journal.com
A monthly guide to natural dog care and training.

Websites

Canine University
www.canineuniversity.com

DogWise
www.dogwise.com

Karen Pryor's Website
www.clickertraining.com

William Campbell's Website
www.webtrail.com/petbehavior/index.html

Index

V

W

Other titles in the series
EVERYTHING
YOU NEED TO KNOW ABOUT...

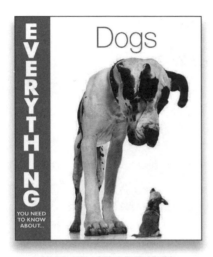

£9.99 ISBN-978-0-7153-2967-2

£9.99 ISBN- 978-0-7153-2062-4

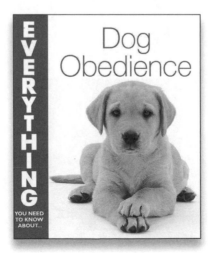

£9.99 ISBN-978-0-7153-2839-2

THE
EVERYTHING
Dog Breed Guides

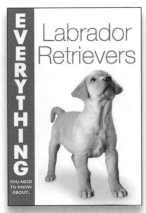

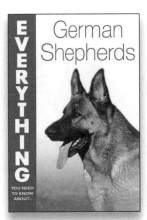

£7.99 ISBN- 978-0-7153-2331-1   **£7.99** ISBN: 978-0-7153-2493-6

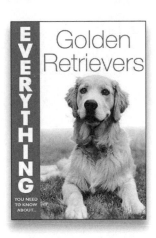

£7.99 ISBN-1978-0-7153-2494-3